W9-BYM-381

our best KNIT BABY AFGHANS

Book 2

*W*ith the first volume of Our Best Knit Baby Afghans *(Leisure Arts book #3219),* we were thrilled to present its 33 adorable patterns by some of America's most talented designers. A decade later, thousands of knitters have created those stunning afghans for the babies in their lives—and now we're delighted to bring you a second volume of our best knit blankets for newborns, infants, and toddlers! Thirty-four classic designs include ripples, chevrons, diagonal elements, lacy looks, and other exciting textures. The warmth and softness of each is destined to charm wee folk and their moms for years to come.

LEISURE ARTS, INC.
Little Rock, Arkansas

EDITORIAL STAFF

Editor-in-Chief: Susan White Sullivan
Knit and Crochet Publications Director: Debra Nettles
Special Projects Director: Susan Frantz Wiles
Senior Prepress Director: Mark Hawkins
Art Publications Director: Rhonda Shelby
Technical Editor: Linda Daley
Contributing Editors: Sarah J. Green and Cathy Hardy
Editorial Writer: Susan McManus Johnson
Art Category Manager: Lora Puls
Graphic Artists: Jacob Casleton and Janie Wright
Imaging Technicians: Brian Hall, Stephanie Johnson,
   and Mark R. Potter
Photography Manager: Katherine Laughlin
Contributing Photographer: Ken West
Contributing Photo Stylist: Sondra Daniel
Publishing Systems Administrator: Becky Riddle
Publishing Systems Assistant: Clint Hanson
Mac IT Specialist: Robert Young

BUSINESS STAFF

Vice President and Chief Operations Officer:
   Tom Siebenmorgen
Director of Finance and Administration: Laticia Mull Dittrich
Vice President, Sales and Marketing: Pam Stebbins
Sales Director: Martha Adams
Marketing Director: Margaret Reinold
Creative Services Director: Jeff Curtis
Information Technology Director: Hermine Linz
Controller: Francis Caple
Vice President, Operations: Jim Dittrich
Comptroller, Operations: Rob Thieme
Retail Customer Service Manager: Stan Raynor
Print Production Manager: Fred F. Pruss

Copyright © 2010 Leisure Arts, Inc., 5701 Ranch Drive, Little Rock, AR 72223-9633. All rights reserved. This publication is protected under federal copyright laws. Reproduction of this publication or any other Leisure Arts publication, including publications which are out of print, is prohibited unless specifically authorized. This includes, but is not limited to, any form of reproduction or distribution on or through the Internet, including posting, scanning, or e-mail transmission. We have made every effort to ensure that these instructions are accurate and complete. We cannot, however, be responsible for human error, typographical mistakes, or variations in individual work. Visit our Web site at **www.leisurearts.com**. U.S.A.

Library of Congress Control Number: 2010923137
ISBN-13: 978-1-60900-032-5

10 9 8 7 6 5 4 3 2 1

Table Of Contents

Aurora

Design by C. Strohmeyer

Finished Size: 32″ x 40″ (81.5 cm x 101.5 cm)

MATERIALS

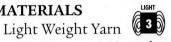

Light Weight Yarn
    13 ounces, 1,010 yards
        (370 grams, 969 meters)
    29″ (73.5 cm) Circular knitting needle,
        size 8 (5 mm) **or** size needed for gauge
    Crochet hook, size H (5 mm)

GAUGE: In Stockinette Stitch,
            18 sts and 28 rows = 4″ (10 cm)

Techniques used:
- YO *(Figs. 4a & b, page 75)*
- K2 tog *(Fig. 8, page 76)*
- SSK *(Figs. 10a-c, page 77)*
- P2 tog *(Fig. 11, page 77)*
- P2 tog tbl *(Fig. 12, page 77)*
- P3 tog *(Fig. 18, page 79)*
- Basic Crochet Stitches *(Figs. 22-25b, page 80)*

AFGHAN
Cast on 149 sts.

Rows 1-18: Knit across.

Row 19: K 10, purl across to last 10 sts, K 10.

Row 20 (Right side)**:** Knit across.

Rows 21-25: Repeat Rows 19 and 20 twice, then repeat Row 19 once **more**.

Row 26: K 16, K2 tog, YO, K1, YO, SSK, (K2, K2 tog, YO, K1, YO, SSK) across to last 16 sts, K 16.

Row 27: K 10, P5, (P2 tog tbl, YO, P3, YO, P2 tog) across to last 15 sts, P5, K 10.

Row 28: K 16, YO, SSK, K1, K2 tog, (YO, K2, YO, SSK, K1, K2 tog) across to last 16 sts, YO, K 16.

Row 29: K 10, P7, YO, P3 tog, (YO, P4, YO, P3 tog) across to last 17 sts, YO, P7, K 10.

Rows 30-45: Repeat Rows 26-29, 4 times.

Row 46: K 16, K2 tog, YO, K1, YO, SSK, (K9, K2 tog, YO, K1, YO, SSK) across to last 16 sts, K 16.

Row 47: K 10, P5, P2 tog tbl, YO, P3, YO, P2 tog, (P7, P2 tog tbl, YO, P3, YO, P2 tog) across to last 15 sts, P5, K 10.

Row 48: K 16, YO, SSK, K1, K2 tog, (YO, K9, YO, SSK, K1, K2 tog) across to last 16 sts, YO, K 16.

Row 49: K 10, P7, YO, P3 tog, (YO, P 11, YO, P3 tog) across to last 17 sts, YO, P7, K 10.

Repeat Rows 46-49 for pattern until Afghan measures approximately 34″ (86.5 cm) from cast on edge, ending by working Row 49.

Next 20 Rows: Repeat Rows 26-29, 5 times.

Next Row: Knit across.

Next Row: K 10, purl across to last 10 sts, K 10.

Next 6 Rows: Repeat last 2 rows, 3 times.

Last 17 Rows: Knit across.

Bind off all sts in knit; do **not** finish off.

TRIM

With **right** side facing, slip loop from needle onto crochet hook; ch 1, sc in first st, ch 3, sc in next st, ★ skip next 2 sts, dc in next st, (ch 1, dc in same st) 4 times, skip next 2 sts, sc in next st, ch 3, sc in next st; repeat from ★ across; finish off.

With **right** side facing and working across bottom edge, join yarn with slip st in first st; work same as top edge.

Baby Cables

◖■▢▢▷ **EASY +**   *Design by Kay Meadors*

Finished Size: 35^1/$_2$" x 46" (90 cm x 117 cm)

MATERIALS

Light Weight Yarn
White - 21 ounces, 1,930 yards
(600 grams, 1,765 meters)
Pink - 11 ounces, 1,010 yards
(310 grams, 924 meters)
29" (73.5 cm) Circular knitting needles,
sizes 10 (6 mm) **and** 10^1/$_2$ (6.5 mm) **or**
sizes needed for gauge

Entire Afghan is worked holding two strands of yarn together.

GAUGE: With larger size needle,
in pattern, 16 sts and 28 rows = 4" (10 cm)

STITCH GUIDE

CABLE (uses next 3 sts)
Slip next 2 sts onto cable needle and hold in **back** of work, knit next st from left needle, K2 from cable needle.

AFGHAN

With smaller size needle and White, cast on 141 sts.

Rows 1-7: Knit across.

Change to larger size needle.

Row 8 (Right side): K9, work Cable, (K5, work Cable) across to last 9 sts, K9.

Row 9: K4, purl across to last 4 sts, K4.

When instructed to slip a stitch, always slip as if to **purl**.

Row 10: Drop White; slip 4, with Pink K5, (slip 3, K5) across to last 4 sts, leave last 4 sts unworked.

Row 11: Turn; K5, (WYF slip 3, WYB K5) across to last 4 sts, WYF drop Pink, slip 4.

Carry yarn not being used **loosely** along inside edge.

Row 12: With White K9, work Cable, (K5, work Cable) across to last 9 sts, K9.

Row 13: K4, purl across to last 4 sts, K4.

Repeat Rows 10-13 for pattern until Afghan measures approximately 45" (114.5 cm) from cast on edge, ending by working Row 12; cut Pink.

Change to smaller size needle.

Last 7 Rows: Knit across.

Bind off all sts in knit.

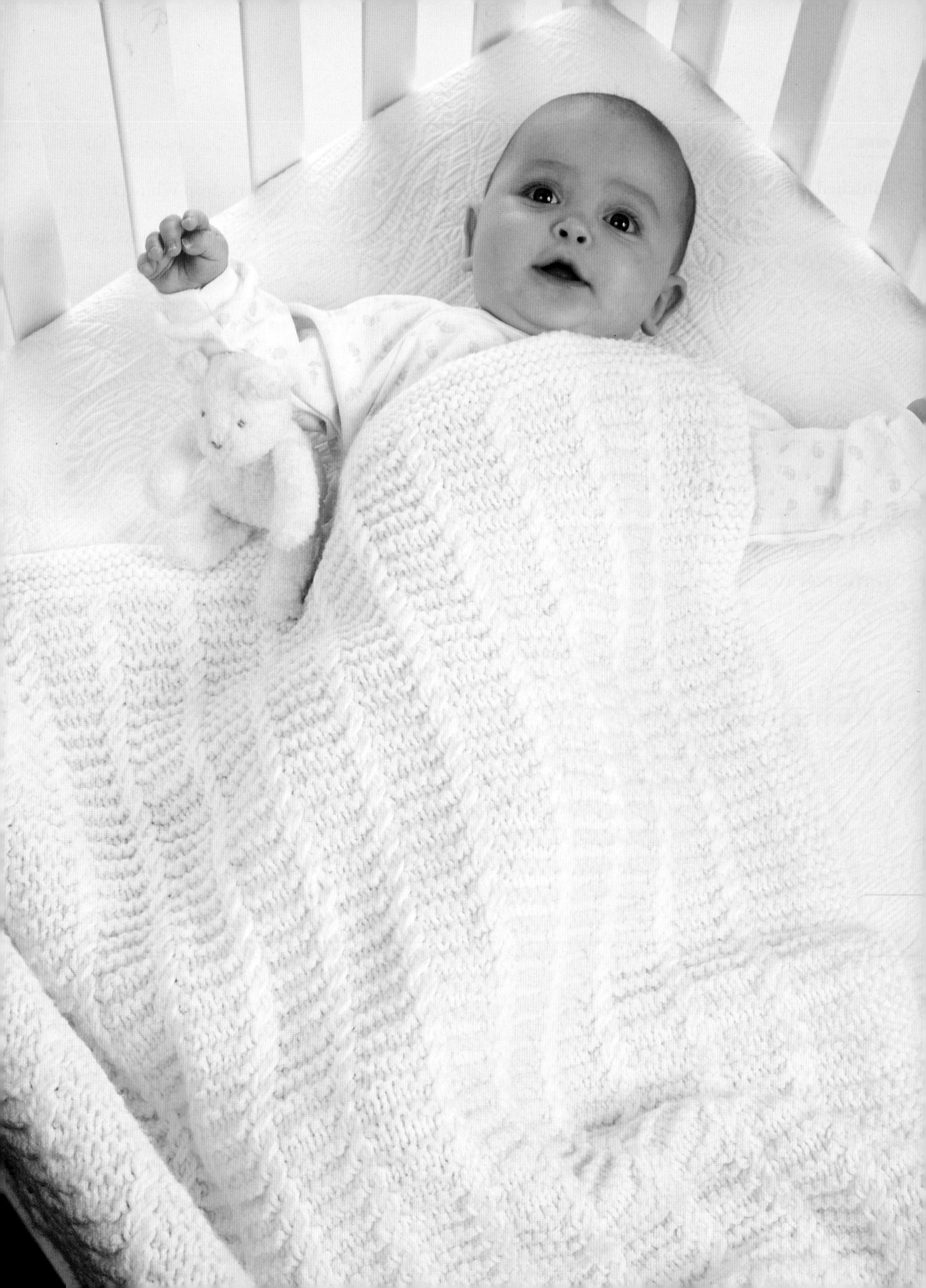

Baby Trellis

☐☐☐☐ EASY

Design by Kay Meadors

Finished Size: 36¼" x 47" (92 cm x 119.5 cm)

MATERIALS

Light Weight Yarn
   White - 25½ ounces, 2,345 yards
      (720 grams, 2,144 meters)
   Yellow - 6¼ ounces, 575 yards
      (180 grams, 526 meters)
   29" (73.5 cm) Circular knitting needles,
      sizes 10 (6 mm) **and** 10½ (6.5 mm) **or**
      sizes needed for gauge

Entire Afghan is worked holding two strands of yarn together.

GAUGE: With larger size needle,
      in pattern, 11 sts = 3" (7.5 cm)
      and 26 rows = 4" (10 cm)

STITCH GUIDE

K1 WITH STRANDS BELOW
Insert tip of right needle from **front** to **back** under both double strands of Yellow below and knit strands together with the next st on the left needle.

AFGHAN
With smaller size needle and White, cast on 133 sts.

Rows 1-7: Knit across.

Change to larger size needle.

Row 8 (Right side)**:** Knit across.

Row 9: K4, purl across to last 4 sts, K4.

Both side borders of Afghan are worked at the same time, using separate yarn for **each** side. When instructed to slip a stitch, slip as if to **purl**.

Row 10: K4 (side border), drop White *(Fig. 20, page 79)*; with Yellow K4, WYF slip 3, (WYB K3, WYF slip 3) across to last 8 sts, WYB K4, drop Yellow; with next White K4.

Row 11: K4, WYF drop White; with Yellow P4, WYB slip 3, (WYF P3, WYB slip 3) across to last 8 sts, WYF P4, cut Yellow; with next White K4.

Row 12: Knit across to last 4 sts, drop White; with next White K4.

Row 13: K4, WYF drop White; with next White purl across to last 4 sts, K4.

Row 14: K9, (K1 with strands below, K5) across to last 4 sts, drop White; with next White K4.

Row 15: K4, WYF drop White; with next White purl across to last 4 sts, K4.

Row 16: K4, drop White; with Yellow K1, WYF slip 3, (WYB K3, WYF slip 3) across to last 5 sts, WYB K1, drop Yellow; with next White K4.

Row 17: K4, WYF drop White; with Yellow P1, WYB slip 3, (WYF P3, WYB slip 3) across to last 5 sts, WYF P1, cut Yellow; with next White K4.

Row 18: Knit across to last 4 sts, drop White; with next White K4.

Row 19: K4, WYF drop White; with next White purl across to last 4 sts, K4.

Row 20: K6, K1 with strands below, (K5, K1 with strands below) across to last 6 sts, K2, drop White; with next White K4.

Row 21: K4, WYF drop White; with next White purl across to last 4 sts, K4.

Row 22: K4, drop White; with Yellow K4, WYF slip 3, (WYB K3, WYF slip 3) across to last 8 sts, WYB K4, drop Yellow; with next White K4.

Repeat Rows 11-22 for pattern until Afghan measures approximately 46" (117 cm) from cast on edge, ending by working Row 14.

Change to smaller size needle.

Next Row: K4, WYF cut White; with next White knit across.

Last 6 Rows: Knit across.

Bind off all sts in knit.

Beloved Blue

 EASY

Design by Carole Prior

Finished Size: 36″ x 45″ (91.5 cm x 114.5 cm)

MATERIALS

Medium Weight Yarn
36 ounces, 2,100 yards
(1,020 grams, 1,920 meters)
29″ (73.5 cm) Circular knitting needle,
size 10¹/₂ (6.5 mm) **or** size needed for gauge

Afghan is worked holding two strands of yarn together.

GAUGE: In pattern,
15 sts and 21 rows = 4¹/₂″ (11.5 cm)

AFGHAN

Cast on 113 sts.

Rows 1-5: Knit across.

Row 6 (Right side)**:** K7, P3, (K3, P3) across to last 7 sts, K7.

Row 7: K4, P3, (K3, P3) across to last 4 sts, K4.

Row 8: K7, P3, (K3, P3) across to last 7 sts, K7.

Rows 9 and 10: K4, P3, (K3, P3) across to last 4 sts, K4.

Row 11: K7, P3, (K3, P3) across to last 7 sts, K7.

Row 12: K4, P3, (K3, P3) across to last 4 sts, K4.

Rows 13 and 14: K7, P3, (K3, P3) across to last 7 sts, K7.

Repeat Rows 7-14 for pattern until Afghan measures approximately 44″ (112 cm) from cast on edge, ending by working Row 9 or Row 13.

Last 5 Rows: Knit across.

Bind off all sts in knit.

Bobbles

Design by Carole Prior

Finished Size: 35″ x 42″ (89 cm x 106.5 cm)

MATERIALS
Light Weight Yarn
   17 ounces, 1,395 yards
     (480 grams, 1,276 meters)
   29″ (73.5 cm) Circular knitting needle,
     size 8 (5 mm) **or** size needed for gauge

GAUGE: In Stockinette Stitch,
       20 sts and 26 rows = 4″ (10 cm)

Techniques used:
- YO *(Fig. 4a, page 75)*
- K2 tog *(Fig. 8, page 76)*
- SSK *(Figs. 10a-c, page 77)*
- Slip 1 as if to **knit**, K2 tog, PSSO *(Figs. 14a & b, page 78)*

STITCH GUIDE

BOBBLE (uses one st)
(K, P, K) **all** in next st, (**turn**, K3) twice, slip second and third sts from right needle **over** first st.

AFGHAN
Cast on 161 sts.

Rows 1-6: K1, (P1, K1) across.

Row 7 AND ALL WRONG SIDE ROWS: K1, (P1, K1) twice, purl across to last 5 sts, K1, (P1, K1) twice.

Row 8: (K1, P1) twice, K3, ★ K2 tog, K1, (YO, K1) twice, SSK, K3; repeat from ★ across to last 4 sts, (P1, K1) twice.

Row 10: (K1, P1) twice, K2, K2 tog, K1, YO, K3, YO, K1, SSK, ★ K1, K2 tog, K1, YO, K3, YO, K1, SSK; repeat from ★ across to last 6 sts, K2, (P1, K1) twice.

When instructed to slip a stitch, always slip as if to knit.

Row 12: (K1, P1) twice, K1, K2 tog, K1, YO, K5, YO, K1, ★ slip 1, K2 tog, PSSO, K1, YO, K5, YO, K1; repeat from ★ across to last 7 sts, SSK, K1, (P1, K1) twice.

Row 14: (K1, P1) twice, K2, YO, K1, SSK, K1, work Bobble, K1, K2 tog, K1, ★ (YO, K1) twice, SSK, K1, work Bobble, K1, K2 tog, K1; repeat from ★ across to last 6 sts, YO, K2, (P1, K1) twice.

Row 16: (K1, P1) twice, K3, ★ YO, K1, SSK, K1, K2 tog, K1, YO, K3; repeat from ★ across to last 4 sts, (P1, K1) twice.

Row 18: (K1, P1) twice, K4, YO, K1, slip 1, K2 tog, PSSO, K1, ★ YO, K5, YO, K1, slip 1, K2 tog, PSSO, K1; repeat from ★ across to last 8 sts, YO, K4, (P1, K1) twice.

Row 20: (K1, P1) twice, K3, K2 tog, K1, (YO, K1) twice, SSK, ★ K1, work Bobble, K1, K2 tog, K1, (YO, K1) twice, SSK; repeat from ★ across to last 7 sts, K3, (P1, K1) twice.

Repeat Rows 9-20 for pattern until Afghan measures approximately 41″ (104 cm) from cast on edge, ending by working Row 19.

Next 6 Rows: K1, (P1, K1) across.

Bind off all sts in pattern.

Chevron Ripple

▆■□□ EASY

Design by Melissa Leapman

Finished Size: 37" x 49" (94 cm x 124.5 cm)

MATERIALS

Medium Weight Yarn
22 ounces, 1,445 yards
(620 grams, 1,321 meters)
29" (73.5 cm) Circular knitting needles,
sizes 8 (5 mm) **and** 10 (6 mm) **or** sizes needed
for gauge

GAUGE: With larger size needle, in pattern,
16 sts and 16 rows = 3" (7.5 cm)
In Stockinette Stitch, 18 sts = 4" (10 cm)

Techniques used:
• YO *(Fig. 4a, page 75)*
• K2 tog *(Fig. 8, page 76)*
• SSK *(Figs. 10a-c, page 77)*

AFGHAN
With smaller size needle, cast on 196 sts.

Rows 1-6: Knit across.

Change to larger size needle.

Row 7 (Right side)**:** K3, YO, K5, SSK, K2 tog, K5,
(YO, K2, YO, K5, SSK, K2 tog, K5) across to last 3 sts,
YO, K3.

Row 8: K3, purl across to last 3 sts, K3.

Row 9: K3, YO, K5, SSK, K2 tog, K5, (YO, K2, YO, K5,
SSK, K2 tog, K5) across to last 3 sts, YO, K3.

Rows 10 and 11: Repeat Rows 8 and 9.

Row 12: Knit across.

Repeat Rows 7-12 for pattern until Afghan measures
approximately 48¹/₄" (122.5 cm) from cast on edge,
ending by working Row 11.

Change to smaller size needle.

Last 6 Rows: Knit across.

Bind off all sts in knit.

Elaine

EASY

Design by Melissa Leapman

Finished Size: 36" x 48" (91.5 cm x 122 cm)

MATERIALS

Medium Weight Yarn
   21 ounces, 1,015 yards
     (600 grams, 928 meters)
   29" (73.5 cm) Circular knitting needle,
     size 10 (6 mm) **or** size needed for gauge

GAUGE: In Stockinette Stitch,
      16 sts and 22 rows = 4" (10 cm)

Techniques used:
- YO *(Fig. 4a, page 75)*
- Slip 2 tog as if to **knit**, K1, P2SSO *(Figs. 16a & b, page 78)*

AFGHAN
Cast on 145 sts.

Rows 1-7: Knit across.

Row 8: K4, purl across to last 4 sts, K4.

Row 9 (Right side)**:** Knit across.

Row 10: K4, purl across to last 4 sts, K4.

Row 11: K6, P3, (K7, P3) across to last 6 sts, K6.

Row 12: K4, P2, K3, (P7, K3) across to last 6 sts, P2, K4.

Row 13: K6, YO, slip 2 tog, K1, P2SSO, (YO, K7, YO, slip 2 tog, K1, P2SSO) across to last 6 sts, YO, K6.

Row 14: K4, purl across to last 4 sts, K4.

Row 15: Knit across.

Row 16: K4, purl across to last 4 sts, K4.

Row 17: Knit across.

Row 18: K4, purl across to last 4 sts, K4.

Row 19: K 11, P3, (K7, P3) across to last 11 sts, K 11.

Row 20: K4, P7, (K3, P7) across to last 4 sts, K4.

Row 21: K 11, YO, slip 2 tog, K1, P2SSO, (YO, K7, YO slip 2 tog, K1, P2SSO) across to last 11 sts, YO, K 11.

Row 22: K4, purl across to last 4 sts, K4.

Row 23: Knit across.

Repeat Rows 8-23 for pattern until Afghan measures approximately 47" (119.5 cm) from cast on edge, ending by working Row 16.

Last 7 Rows: Knit across.

Bind off all sts in knit.

Elise

EASY +

Design by Melissa Leapman

Finished Size: 37" x 49" (94 cm x 124.5 cm)

MATERIALS

Medium Weight Yarn
  22 ounces, 1,065 yards
    (620 grams, 974 meters)
29" (73.5 cm) Circular knitting needle,
  size 10 (6 mm) **or** size needed for gauge

GAUGE: In Stockinette Stitch,
      16 sts and 22 rows = 4" (10 cm)

Techniques used:
• YO *(Fig. 4a, page 75)*
• SSK *(Figs. 10a-c, page 77)*

AFGHAN

Cast on 147 sts.

Rows 1-6: Knit across.

Row 7 (Right side): K5, YO, SSK, (K4, YO, SSK) across to last 8 sts, K8.

Row 8: K4, purl across to last 4 sts, K4.

Row 9: K6, YO, SSK, (K4, YO, SSK) across to last 7 sts, K7.

Row 10: K4, purl across to last 4 sts, K4.

Row 11: K7, YO, SSK, (K4, YO, SSK) across to last 6 sts, K6.

Row 12: K4, purl across to last 4 sts, K4.

Row 13: K8, YO, SSK, (K4, YO, SSK) across to last 5 sts, K5.

Row 14: K4, purl across to last 4 sts, K4.

Row 15: K9, (YO, SSK, K4) across.

Row 16: K4, purl across to last 4 sts, K4.

Row 17: K 10, YO, SSK, (K4, YO, SSK) across to last 9 sts, K9.

Row 18: K4, purl across to last 4 sts, K4.

Repeat Rows 7-18 for pattern until Afghan measures approximately 48" (122 cm) from cast on edge, ending by working Row 15.

Last 6 Rows: Knit across.

Bind off all sts in knit.

Ella

Design by Melissa Leapman

Finished Size: 37" x 49" (94 cm x 124.5 cm)

MATERIALS

Medium Weight Yarn
24 ounces, 1,160 yards
(680 grams, 1,061 meters)
29" (73.5 cm) Circular knitting needle,
size 10 (6 mm) **or** size needed for gauge

GAUGE: In Stockinette Stitch,
16 sts and 22 rows = 4" (10 cm)

Techniques used:
- YO *(Figs. 4a & b, page 75)*
- K2 tog *(Fig. 8, page 76)*
- P2 tog *(Fig. 11, page 77)*
- SSK *(Figs. 10a-c, page 77)*
- Slip 1 as if to **knit**, K2 tog, PSSO *(Figs. 14a & b, page 78)*

STITCH GUIDE

BOBBLE (uses one st)
(K1, YO, K1) **all** in next st, **turn**; P1, (P1, YO, P1) **all** in next st, P1, **turn**; K5, **turn**; P2 tog, P1, P2 tog, **turn**; slip 1, K2 tog, PSSO.

AFGHAN
Cast on 147 sts.

Rows 1-6: Knit across.

Row 7 (Right side): K8, K2 tog, YO, K1, YO, SSK, (K 13, K2 tog, YO, K1, YO, SSK) across to last 8 sts, K8.

Row 8: K4, purl across to last 4 sts, K4.

Row 9: K7, K2 tog, K1, (YO, K1) twice, SSK, ★ K 11, K2 tog, K1, (YO, K1) twice, SSK; repeat from ★ across to last 7 sts, K7.

Row 10: K4, purl across to last 4 sts, K4.

Row 11: K6, K2 tog, K2, YO, K1, YO, K2, SSK, (K9, K2 tog, K2, YO, K1, YO, K2, SSK) across to last 6 sts, K6.

Row 12: K4, purl across to last 4 sts, K4.

Row 13: K5, K2 tog, K3, YO, K1, YO, K3, SSK, (K7, K2 tog, K3, YO, K1, YO, K3, SSK) across to last 5 sts, K5.

Row 14: K4, purl across to last 4 sts, K4.

Row 15: K 10, work Bobble, (K 17, work Bobble) across to last 10 sts, K 10.

Row 16: K4, purl across to last 4 sts, K4.

Row 17: K 17, K2 tog, YO, K1, YO, SSK, (K 13, K2 tog, YO, K1, YO, SSK) across to last 17 sts, K 17.

Row 18: K4, purl across to last 4 sts, K4.

Row 19: K 16, K2 tog, K1, (YO, K1) twice, SSK, ★ K 11, K2 tog, K1, (YO, K1) twice, SSK; repeat from ★ across to last 16 sts, K 16.

Row 20: K4, purl across to last 4 sts, K4.

Row 21: K 15, K2 tog, K2, YO, K1, YO, K2, SSK, (K9, K2 tog, K2, YO, K1, YO, K2, SSK) across to last 15 sts, K 15.

Row 22: K4, purl across to last 4 sts, K4.

Row 23: K 14, K2 tog, K3, YO, K1, YO, K3, SSK, (K7, K2 tog, K3, YO, K1, YO, K3, SSK) across to last 14 sts, K 14.

Row 24: K4, purl across to last 4 sts, K4.

Row 25: K 19, work Bobble, (K 17, work Bobble) across to last 19 sts, K 19.

Row 26: K4, purl across to last 4 sts, K4.

Repeat Rows 7-26 for pattern until Afghan measures approximately 48″ (122 cm) from cast on edge, ending by working Row 16.

Last 7 Rows: Knit across.

Bind off all sts in knit.

Estelle

EASY +

Design by Melissa Leapman

Finished Size: 37″ x 49″ (94 cm x 124.5 cm)

MATERIALS

Medium Weight Yarn
24 ounces, 1,160 yards
   (680 grams, 1,061 meters)
29″ (73.5 cm) Circular knitting needle,
   size 10 (6 mm) **or** size needed for gauge

GAUGE: In Stockinette Stitch,
          16 sts and 22 rows = 4″ (10 cm)

Techniques used:
• YO *(Figs. 4c & d, page 75)*
• P3 tog *(Fig. 18, page 79)*

AFGHAN

Cast on 147 sts.

Rows 1-7: Knit across.

Row 8: K4, purl across to last 4 sts, K4.

Row 9 (Right side)**:** K5, YO, P1, P3 tog, P1, (YO, K1, YO, P1, P3 tog, P1) across to last 5 sts, YO, K5.

Row 10: K4, purl across to last 4 sts, K4.

Row 11: Knit across.

Row 12: K4, purl across to last 4 sts, K4.

Repeat Rows 9-12 for pattern until Afghan measures approximately 48″ (122 cm) from cast on edge, ending by working Row 10.

Last 7 Rows: Knit across.

Bind off all sts in knit.

Eyelet

EASY

Design by Jeannine LaRoche

Finished Size: 35" x 36" (89 cm x 91.5 cm)

MATERIALS

Light Weight Yarn
   Pink - 11 ounces, 1,010 yards
      (310 grams, 924 meters)
   White - 2 ounces, 185 yards
      (60 grams, 169 meters)
   29" (73.5 cm) Circular knitting needle,
      size 7 (4.5 mm) **or** size needed for gauge

GAUGE: In Stockinette Stitch,
         20 sts and 24 rows = 4" (10 cm)

Techniques used:
• YO (*Fig. 4a, page 75*)
• K2 tog (*Fig. 8, page 76*)

AFGHAN

With Pink, cast on 175 sts.

Rows 1-8: Knit across.

Row 9: K5, purl across to last 5 sts, K5.

Row 10 (Right side): Knit across.

Rows 11-14: Repeat Rows 9 and 10 twice.

Row 15: Knit across.

To avoid cutting yarn, carry yarn not being used **loosely** along edge, twisting every other row on **wrong** side, one stitch in.

Row 16: With White, knit across.

Row 17 (Eyelet row): K6, (YO, K2 tog) across to last 5 sts, K5.

Rows 18-20: With Pink, knit across.

Repeat Rows 9-20 for pattern until Afghan measures approximately 35" (89 cm) from cast on edge, ending by working Row 14; cut White.

Next 7 Rows: Knit across.

Bind off all sts in knit.

Eyelet Lace

INTERMEDIATE

Design by Donna Inman

Finished Size: 30″ x 40″ (76 cm x 101.5 cm)

MATERIALS

Medium Weight Yarn
  13$\frac{1}{2}$ ounces, 930 yards
  (380 grams, 850 meters)
29″ (73.5 cm) Circular knitting needle,
  size 9 (5.5 mm) **or** size needed for gauge
2 Stitch holders
Yarn needle

GAUGE: In Garter Stitch,
  16 sts = 4″ (10 cm)

Techniques used:
• YO *(Fig. 4a, page 75)*
• K2 tog *(Fig. 8, page 76)*
• Slip 1 as if to **knit**, K1, PSSO *(Fig. 9, page 77)*
• Slip 1 as if to **knit**, K2 tog, PSSO *(Figs. 14a & b, page 78)*

BOTTOM BORDER

Cast on 119 sts.

Rows 1-8: Knit across.

Row 9: K8 and slip these sts onto st holder (Border), knit across to last 8 sts, slip last 8 sts onto second st holder (Border): 103 sts.

CENTER PANEL

When instructed to slip a stitch, always slip as if to knit.

Row 1: K1, ★ K2 tog, YO, K1, YO, slip 1, K1, PSSO, K1; repeat from ★ across.

Row 2 AND ALL WRONG SIDE ROWS: Purl across.

Row 3: K2 tog, ★ YO, K3, YO, slip 1, K2 tog, PSSO; repeat from ★ across to last 5 sts, YO, K3, YO, K2 tog.

Row 5: K2, ★ YO, slip 1, K2 tog, PSSO, YO, K3; repeat from ★ across to last 5 sts, YO, slip 1, K2 tog, PSSO, YO, K2.

Row 7: K1, ★ K2 tog, YO, K1, YO, slip 1, K1, PSSO, K1; repeat from ★ across.

Repeat Rows 2-7 for pattern until piece measures approximately 38$\frac{1}{2}$″ (98 cm) from cast on edge, ending by working a **right** side row.

With yarn needle, thread a long length of yarn through remaining sts; tie ends together.

SIDE BORDER

With **wrong** side facing, slip sts from left side st holder onto needle. Knit every row until Border measures same as Center Panel, ending by working a **right** side row; slip sts onto st holder.

Sew Border to Center Panel.

With **right** side facing, work second Side Border same as first side.

TOP BORDER

With **wrong** side facing, slip all sts onto needle.

Rows 1-9: Knit across.

Bind off all sts in knit.

Eyelet Ripple

EASY

Design by Melissa Leapman

Finished Size: 36¹/₂" x 47" (92.5 cm x 119.5 cm)

MATERIALS

Medium Weight Yarn
  17 ounces, 1,115 yards
    (480 grams, 1,020 meters)
  29" (73.5 cm) Circular knitting needles,
    sizes 8 (5 mm) **and** 10 (6 mm) **or** sizes needed
    for gauge

GAUGE: With larger size needle, in pattern,
        24 sts and 25 rows = 5" (12.75 cm)
        In Stockinette Stitch, 18 sts = 4" (10 cm)

Techniques used:
- YO *(Fig. 4a, page 75)*
- K2 tog *(Fig. 8, page 76)*
- SSK *(Figs. 10a-c, page 77)*
- Slip 2 tog as if to **knit**, K1, P2SSO *(Figs. 16a & b, page 78)*

AFGHAN
With smaller size needle, cast on 175 sts.

Rows 1-6: Knit across.

Change to larger size needle.

Row 7 (Right side)**:** K4, YO, K4, slip 2 tog, K1, P2SSO, K4, ★ YO, K1, YO, K4, slip 2 tog, K1, P2SSO, K4; repeat from ★ across to last 4 sts, YO, K4.

Row 8: K3, purl across to last 3 sts, K3.

Rows 9-14: Repeat Rows 7 and 8, 3 times.

Row 15: K4, (YO, SSK) twice, YO, slip 2 tog, K1, P2SSO, (YO, K2 tog) twice, ★ YO, K1, (YO, SSK) twice, YO, slip 2 tog, K1, P2SSO, (YO, K2 tog) twice; repeat from ★ across to last 4 sts, YO, K4.

Row 16: K3, purl across to last 3 sts, K3.

Repeat Rows 7-16 for pattern until Afghan measures approximately 46¹/₄" (117.5 cm) from cast on edge, ending by working Row 13.

Change to smaller size needle.

Last 6 Rows: Knit across.

Bind off all sts in knit.

Kitten

INTERMEDIATE

Design by Cynthia Guggemos

Finished Size: 36" (91.5 cm) square

MATERIALS

Light Weight Yarn
15 ounces, 1,375 yards
(430 grams, 1,257 meters)
29" (73.5 cm) Circular knitting needle,
size 7 (4.5 mm) **or** size needed for gauge
Markers
Yarn needle

GAUGE: In Seed Stitch,
20 sts and 35 rows = 4" (10 cm)
In Stockinette Stitch,
20 sts and 28 rows = 4" (10 cm)

Techniques used:
• YO *(Fig. 4a, page 75)*
• K2 tog *(Fig. 8, page 76)*
• SSK *(Figs. 10a-c, page 77)*
• Slip 1 as if to **knit**, K2 tog, PSSO *(Figs.14a & b, page 78)*

BOTTOM BAND
Cast on 177 sts.

Row 1: (K1, P1) across to last st, WYF slip 1 as if to **purl**.

Repeat Row 1 for pattern until Afghan measures approximately 3" (7.5 cm) from cast on edge.

CENTER
Row 1 (Right side)**:** K1, (P1, K1) 7 times, place marker *(see Markers, page 74)*, K1, YO, K2 tog, ★ K3, K2 tog, YO, K1, YO, SSK, K3, YO, K2 tog; repeat from ★ 10 times **more**, K1, place marker, (K1, P1) across to last st, WYF slip 1 as if to **purl**.

Row 2 AND ALL WRONG SIDE ROWS THROUGHOUT CENTER: K1, (P1, K1) across to next marker, purl across to next marker, (K1, P1) across to last st, WYF slip 1 as if to **purl**.

Row 3: K1, (P1, K1) across to next marker, K1, SSK, (YO, K2, K2 tog, YO, K3, YO, SSK, K2, SSK) across to within one st of next marker, YO, K2, P1, (K1, P1) across to last st, WYF slip 1 as if to **purl**.

Row 5: K1, (P1, K1) across to next marker, K1, YO, K2 tog, ★ K3, YO, SSK, K1, K2 tog, YO, K3, YO, K2 tog; repeat from ★ across to within one st of next marker, K2, P1, (K1, P1) across to last st, WYF slip 1 a if to **purl**.

Row 7: K1, (P1, K1) across to next marker, K1, SSK, ★ YO, K4, YO, slip 1, K2 tog, PSSO, YO, K4, SSK; repeat from ★ across to within one st of next marker, YO, K2, P1, (K1, P1) across to last st, WYF slip 1 as if to **purl**.

Row 9: K1, (P1, K1) across to next marker, K1, YO, K2 tog, ★ K3, K2 tog, YO, K1, YO, SSK, K3, YO, K2 tog; repeat from ★ across to within one st of next marker, K2, P1, (K1, P1) across to last st, WYF slip 1 a if to **purl**.

Repeat Rows 2-9 for pattern until Afghan measures approximately 33" (84 cm) from cast on edge, ending by working Row 8 and removing markers on last row.

TOP BAND
Row 1: (K1, P1) across to last st, WYF slip 1 as if to **purl**.

Repeat Row 1 until Afghan measures approximately 36" (91.5 cm) from cast on edge.

Bind off all sts in pattern.

Lacy Ripple

■□□◁ EASY +

Design by Melissa Leapman

Finished Size: 35¹/₂″ x 48″ (90 cm x 122 cm)

MATERIALS

Medium Weight Yarn
  20 ounces, 1,310 yards
    (570 grams, 1,198 meters)
  29″ (73.5 cm) Circular knitting needles,
    sizes 8 (5 mm) **and** 10 (6 mm) **or** sizes needed
    for gauge

GAUGE: With larger size needle, in pattern,
      20 sts and 28 rows = 4¹/₂″ (11.5 cm)
      In Stockinette Stitch, 18 sts = 4″ (10 cm)

Techniques used:
- YO *(Fig. 4a, page 75)*
- K3 tog *(Fig. 17, page 79)*
- Slip 1 as if to **knit**, K2 tog, PSSO *(Figs. 14a & b, page 78)*
- Slip 2 tog as if to **knit**, K3 tog, P2SSO *(Figs. 19a & b, page 79)*

AFGHAN

With smaller size needle, cast on 157 sts.

Rows 1-6: Knit across.

Change to larger size needle.

Row 7 (Right side)**:** Knit across.

Row 8: K3, purl across to last 3 sts, K3.

Row 9: K3, slip 1, K2 tog, PSSO, K1, ★ (YO, K1) 4 times, slip 2 tog, K3 tog, P2SSO, K1; repeat from ★ across to last 10 sts, (YO, K1) 3 times, YO, K3 tog, K4.

Rows 10 and 11: Knit across.

Row 12: K3, purl across to last 3 sts, K3.

Repeat Rows 9-12 for pattern until Afghan measures approximately 47¹/₄″ (120 cm) from cast on edge, ending by working Row 11.

Change to smaller size needle.

Last 6 Rows: Knit across.

Bind off all sts in knit.

Little Lamb

■■□□ EASY

Design by Jeannine LaRoche

Finished Size: 35" x 41" (89 cm x 104 cm)

MATERIALS
Medium Weight Yarn
  21 ounces, 1,185 yards
    (600 grams, 1,084 meters)
  29" (73.5 cm) Circular knitting needle,
    size 10 (6 mm) **or** size needed for gauge

GAUGE: In pattern, 16 sts and 24 rows = 4" (10 cm)
    In Stockinette Stitch,
      16 sts and 22 rows = 4" (10 cm)

Techniques used:
• Knit increase *(Figs. 5a & b, page 76)*
• K2 tog *(Fig. 8, page 76)*

AFGHAN
Cast on 123 sts.

Rows 1-4: Knit across.

Row 5 (Right side): K5, work knit increase, (K6, work knit increase) across to last 5 sts, K5: 140 sts.

Row 6: K5, purl across to last 5 sts, K5.

Row 7: Knit across.

Row 8: K5, purl across to last 5 sts, K5.

Row 9: Knit across.

When instructed to slip a stitch, always slip as if to **purl** with yarn held **loosely** to the back.

Row 10: K7, slip 2, (K2, slip 2) across to last 7 sts, K7.

Row 11: Knit across.

Row 12: K7, slip 2, (K2, slip 2) across to last 7 sts, K7.

Row 13: Knit across.

Repeat Rows 6-13 for pattern until Afghan measures approximately 40" (101.5 cm) from cast on edge, ending by working Row 6.

Decrease Row: K5, K2 tog, (K6, K2 tog) across to last 5 sts, K5: 123 sts.

Last 4 Rows: Knit across.

Bind off remaining sts in knit.

Lollipop

◖◗▭▭▭ EASY +

Finished Size: 31″ (78.5 cm) square

MATERIALS

Light Weight Yarn
  Variegated - 12¹/₂ ounces, 1,235 yards
    (360 grams, 1,129 meters)
  Blue - 11¹/₂ ounces, 910 yards
    (330 grams, 832 meters)
Knitting needles, size 13 (9 mm) **or** size needed
  for gauge
Crochet hook, size H (5 mm)
Yarn needle

Entire Afghan is worked holding two strands of yarn together.

GAUGE: In pattern, 13 sts and 22 rows = 4″ (10 cm)

Techniques used:
• YO (*Fig. 4a, page 75*)
• K2 tog (*Fig. 8, page 76*)
• SSK (*Figs. 10a-c, page 77*)
• Basic Crochet Stitches (*Figs. 22-25b, page 80*)

TRIANGLE SHAPE (Make 4)

With Blue, cast on 3 sts.

Row 1: K3.

Row 2 (Right side)**:** K1, (YO, K1) twice: 5 sts.

Row 3: K5.

Row 4 (Increase row)**:** K1, YO, knit across to last st, YO, K1: 7 sts.

Row 5: Knit across.

Rows 6-19: Repeat Rows 4 and 5, 7 times: 21 sts.

Rows 20-24: With Variegated, repeat Rows 4 and 5 twice, then repeat Row 4 once **more**: 27 sts.

Row 25: Purl across.

Row 26: K1, (YO, SSK) across to last 2 sts, (YO, K1) twice: 29 sts.

Row 27: Purl across.

Rows 28-31: Repeat Rows 4 and 5 twice: 33 sts.

Rows 32-43: With Blue, repeat Rows 4 and 5, 6 times 45 sts.

Rows 44-79: Repeat Rows 20-43 once, then repeat Rows 20-31 once **more**: 81 sts.

Rows 80-93: With Blue, repeat Rows 4 and 5, 7 times 95 sts.

Rows 94-97: With Variegated, repeat Rows 4 and 5 twice: 99 sts.

SCALLOP EDGING

K9, **turn**; K2 tog, K7, **turn**; K2 tog, K6, **turn**; K2 tog, K5, **turn**; K2 tog, K4, **turn**; K2 tog, K3, **turn**; bind off 3 sts, slip remaining st from right needle onto crochet hook; (ch 1, sc) evenly along side of Scallop, ★ ch 1, sc in bar before next st, ch 1, slip loop from hook back to left needle, K2 tog, K7, K2 tog, **turn**; K2 tog, K7, **turn**; K2 tog, K6, **turn**; K2 tog, K5, **turn**; K2 tog, K4, **turn**; K2 tog, K3, **turn**; bind off 3 sts, slip remaining st from right needle onto crochet hook; (ch 1, sc) evenly along side of Scallop; repeat from ★ across; finish off.

Sew Triangles together.

FLOWER

With crochet hook and using 2 strands of Variegated, h 4; join with slip st to form a ring.

Rnd 1: Ch 1, (sc in ring, ch 3) 5 times; join with slip st o first sc: 5 ch-3 sps.

Rnd 2: (Sc, ch 3, 3 dc, sc) in each ch-3 sp around; join with slip st to first sc, finish off: 5 petals.

Sew Flower to center of Afghan.

Pleated Herringbone

Design by Judy S. Lamb

Finished Size: 28¹/₂″ x 36″ (72.5 cm x 91.5 cm)

MATERIALS

Light Weight Yarn
14 ounces, 1,150 yards
(400 grams, 1,052 meters)
29″ (73.5 cm) Circular knitting needle,
size 6 (4 mm) **or** size needed for gauge

GAUGE: In Stockinette Stitch,
22 sts and 28 rows = 4″ (10 cm)

Techniques used:
• YO *(Figs. 4a, 4c & 4d, page 75)*
• K2 tog *(Fig. 8, page 76)*
• SSK *(Figs. 10a-c, page 77)*

BOTTOM BORDER
Cast on 157 sts.

Row 1 (Right side): K1, (YO, K2 tog) across.

Rows 2-4: Knit across.

Rows 5-12: Repeat Rows 1-4 twice.

BODY
Row 1: (SSK, YO) 3 times, P1, (K5, P1) across to last 6 sts, (YO, K2 tog) across.

Row 2: K6, P1, (K1, P3, K1, P1) across to last 6 sts, K6.

Row 3: K8, P1, K1, P1, (K3, P1, K1, P1) across to last 8 sts, K8.

Row 4: K6, P3, K1, (P5, K1) across to last 9 sts, P3, K6.

Row 5: (SSK, YO) 3 times, K2, P1, K1, P1, (K3, P1, K1, P1) across to last 8 sts, K2, (YO, K2 tog) 3 times.

Row 6: K6, P1, (K1, P3, K1, P1) across to last 6 sts, K6.

Row 7: K6, P1, (K5, P1) across to last 6 sts, K6.

Row 8: K6, P1, (K1, P3, K1, P1) across to last 6 sts, K6.

Row 9: (SSK, YO) 3 times, K2, P1, K1, P1, (K3, P1, K1, P1) across to last 8 sts, K2, (YO, K2 tog) 3 times.

Row 10: K6, P3, K1, (P5, K1) across to last 9 sts, P3, K6.

Row 11: K8, P1, K1, P1, (K3, P1, K1, P1) across to last 8 sts, K8.

Row 12: K6, P1, (K1, P3, K1, P1) across to last 6 sts, K6.

Repeat Rows 1-12 for pattern until Afghan measures approximately 34″ (86.5 cm) from cast on edge, ending by working Row 1.

TOP BORDER
Rows 1-3: Knit across.

Rows 4-12: Repeat Rows 1-4 of Bottom Border twice, then repeat Row 1 once **more**.

Bind off all sts in knit.

Precious

Design by Jeannine LaRoche

Finished Size: 35" x 41" (89 cm x 104 cm)

MATERIALS

Medium Weight Yarn
22¼ ounces, 1,255 yards
(630 grams, 1,148 meters)
29" (73.5 cm) Circular knitting needle,
size 10 (6 mm) **or** size needed for gauge

GAUGE: In pattern, 21 sts and 24 rows = 4" (10 cm)
In Stockinette Stitch,
16 sts and 22 rows = 4" (10 cm)

Techniques used:
• Knit increase *(Figs. 5a & b, page 76)*
• K2 tog *(Fig. 8, page 76)*
• YO *(Fig. 4a, page 75)*
• Slip 1 as if to **knit**, K2, PSSO *(Figs. 13a & b, page 78)*

AFGHAN
Cast on 137 sts.

Rows 1-4: Knit across.

Row 5 (Right side)**:** K5, work knit increase, (K2, work knit increase) across to last 5 sts, K5: 180 sts.

Row 6: K5, (YO, slip 1, K2, PSSO) across to last 4 sts, K4.

Row 7: K4, purl across to last 4 sts, K4.

Row 8: K4, slip 1, K2, PSSO, (YO, slip 1, K2, PSSO) across to last 5 sts, YO, K5.

Row 9: K4, purl across to last 4 sts, K4.

Repeat Rows 6-9 for pattern until Afghan measures approximately 40" (101.5 cm) from cast on edge, ending by working a **wrong** side row.

Decrease Row: K5, K2 tog, (K2, K2 tog) across to last 5 sts, K5: 137 sts.

Last 4 Rows: Knit across.

Bind off remaining sts in knit.

Ribbed

Design by Carole Prior

Finished Size: 34" x 42" (86.5 cm x 106.5 cm)

MATERIALS
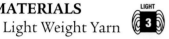
Light Weight Yarn
   14 ounces, 1,105 yards
      (400 grams, 1,010 meters)
   29" (73.5 cm) Circular knitting needle,
      size 8 (5 mm) **or** size needed for gauge

GAUGE: In Stockinette Stitch,
            20 sts and 26 rows = 4" (10 cm)

Techniques used:
• YO *(Fig. 4a, page 75)*
• K2 tog *(Fig. 8, page 76)*
• SSK *(Figs. 10a-c, page 77)*

AFGHAN
Cast on 167 sts.

Row 1 (Wrong side): K1, purl across to last st, K1.

Row 2: K1, (YO, K2 tog) across.

Row 3: K1, purl across to last st, K1.

Row 4: K1, (SSK, YO) across to last 2 sts, K2.

Row 5: K1, purl across to last st, K1.

Rows 6-9: Repeat Rows 2-5.

To work Right Twist 2 (abbreviated RT2) (uses next 2 sts), skip next st on left needle, knit next st, knit skipped st, slip both sts off left needle.

Row 10: K1, (YO, K2 tog) 3 times, P3, (RT2, P3) across to last 7 sts, K1, (YO, K2 tog) 3 times.

Row 11: K1, P6, K3, (P2, K3) across to last 7 sts, P6, K1.

Row 12: K1, (SSK, YO) twice, K2, P3, (RT2, P3) across to last 7 sts, K1, (SSK, YO) twice, K2.

Row 13: K1, P6, K3, (P2, K3) across to last 7 sts, P6, K1.

Repeat Rows 10-13 for pattern until Afghan measures approximately 41" (104 cm) from cast on edge, ending by working Row 13.

Last 8 Rows: Repeat Rows 2-9.

Bind off all sts in knit.

Ribbed Ripple

■■□□ EASY

Design by Melissa Leapman

Finished Size: 35″ x 45″ (89 cm x 114.5 cm)

MATERIALS

Medium Weight Yarn
  18 ounces, 1,180 yards
    (510 grams, 1,079 meters)
  29″ (73.5 cm) Circular knitting needles,
    sizes 8 (5 mm) **and** 10 (6 mm) **or** sizes needed
    for gauge

GAUGE: With larger size needle, in pattern,
      22 sts and 22 rows = 4¹/₂″ (11.5 cm)
      In Stockinette Stitch, 18 sts = 4″ (10 cm)

Techniques used:
• Knit increase *(Figs. 5a & b, page 76)*
• Slip 2 tog as if to **knit**, K1, P2SSO *(Figs. 16a & b, page 78)*

AFGHAN

With smaller size needle, cast on 171 sts.

Rows 1-6: Knit across.

Change to larger size needle.

Row 7 (Right side)**:** K3, work knit increase, K3, slip 2 tog, K1, P2SSO, K3, ★ work knit increase twice, K3, slip 2 tog, K1, P2SSO, K3; repeat from ★ across to last 4 sts, work knit increase, K3.

Row 8: K3, purl across to last 3 sts, K3.

Repeat Rows 7 and 8 for pattern until Afghan measures approximately 44¹/₄″ (112.5 cm) from cast on edge, ending by working Row 7.

Change to smaller size needle.

Last 6 Rows: Knit across.

Bind off all sts in knit.

Sleepy Time

Design by Evelyn A. Clark

Finished Size: 35″ x 45″ (89 cm x 114.5 cm)

MATERIALS

Light Weight Yarn
    Lavender - 8 ounces, 755 yards
      (230 grams, 690 meters)
    White - 8 ounces, 755 yards
      (230 grams, 690 meters)
    29″ (73.5 cm) Circular knitting needles,
      sizes 13 (9 mm) **and** 15 (10 mm) **or**
      sizes needed for gauge

Entire Afghan is made holding one strand of Lavender and one strand of White together.

GAUGE: With larger size needle,
    in Stockinette Stitch,
    11 sts and 14 rows = 4″ (10 cm)

Techniques used:
• YO *(Fig. 4b, page 75)*
• P2 tog *(Fig. 11, page 77)*

AFGHAN

With smaller size needle, cast on 95 sts.

Rows 1-6: K1, (P1, K1) across.

Change to larger size needle.

Row 7: (K1, P1) twice, knit across to last 4 sts, (P1, K1) twice.

Row 8: K1, (P1, K1) twice, P6, K1, (P 11, K1) across to last 11 sts, P6, K1, (P1, K1) twice.

Row 9: (K1, P1) twice, K6, P3, (K9, P3) across to last 10 sts, K6, (P1, K1) twice.

Row 10: K1, (P1, K1) twice, P4, K5, (P7, K5) across to last 9 sts, P4, K1, (P1, K1) twice.

Row 11: (K1, P1) twice, K4, P7, (K5, P7) across to last 8 sts, K4, (P1, K1) twice.

Row 12: K1, (P1, K1) twice, P2, K9, (P3, K9) across to last 7 sts, P2, K1, (P1, K1) twice.

Row 13: (K1, P1) twice, K2, P4, P2 tog, YO, P5, ★ K1, P4, P2 tog, YO, P5; repeat from ★ across to last 6 sts, K2, (P1, K1) twice.

Row 14: K1, (P1, K1) twice, P2, K9, (P3, K9) across to last 7 sts, P2, K1, (P1, K1) twice.

Row 15: (K1, P1) twice, K4, P7, (K5, P7) across to last 8 sts, K4, (P1, K1) twice.

Row 16: K1, (P1, K1) twice, P4, K5, (P7, K5) across to last 9 sts, P4, K1, (P1, K1) twice.

Row 17: (K1, P1) twice, K6, P3, (K9, P3) across to last 10 sts, K6, (P1, K1) twice.

Row 18: K1, (P1, K1) twice, P6, K1, (P 11, K1) across to last 11 sts, P6, K1, (P1, K1) twice.

Row 19: (K1, P1) twice, knit across to last 4 sts, (P1, K1) twice.

Rows 20-151: Repeat Rows 8-19, 11 times.

Change to smaller size needle.

Rows 152-157: K1, (P1, K1) across.

Bind off all sts in pattern.

Snowflake Eyelet

EASY +

Design by Judy Bolin

Finished Size: 32″ x 45″ (81.5 cm x 114.5 cm)

MATERIALS

Light Weight Yarn
   15¹/₂ ounces, 1,265 yards
      (440 grams, 1,157 meters)
   29″ (73.5 cm) Circular knitting needle,
      size 7 (4.5 mm) **or** size needed for gauge
Markers

GAUGE: In Stockinette Stitch,
         22 sts and 30 rows = 4″ (10 cm)

Techniques used:
• YO (*Fig. 4a, page 75*)
• K2 tog (*Fig. 8, page 76*)
• SSK (*Figs. 10a-c, page 77*)
• Slip, slip, K1, P2SSO (*Figs. 15a & b, page 78*)

BORDER
Cast on 175 sts.

Work in Garter Stitch for 2″ (5 cm).

BODY
Row 1 (Wrong side)**:** K 13 (Border), P 45, place marker (*see Markers, page 74*), (K7, P 45, place marker) twice, K 13.

Row 2: † Knit across to next marker, K4, SSK, YO, K1, YO, K2 tog, (K3, SSK, YO, K1, YO, K2 tog) 4 times †, K 11, repeat from † to † once, knit across (Border).

Row 3 AND ALL WRONG SIDE ROWS THROUGH Row 55: K 13, purl across to next marker, (K7, purl across to next marker) twice, knit across.

Row 4: † Knit across to next marker, K5, YO, slip, slip, K1, P2SSO, YO, (K5, YO, slip, slip, K1, P2SSO, YO) 4 times †, K 12, repeat from † to † once, knit across.

Row 6: Repeat Row 2.

Row 8: † Knit across to next marker, SSK, YO, K1, YO, K2 tog, (K3, SSK, YO, K1, YO, K2 tog) 5 times †, K7, repeat from † to † once, knit across.

Row 10: † Knit across to next marker, K1, YO, slip, slip, K1, P2SSO, YO, (K5, YO, slip, slip, K1, P2SSO, YO) 5 times †, K8, repeat from † to † once, knit across.

Row 12: Repeat Row 8.

Rows 14-55: Repeat Rows 2-13, 3 times; then repeat Rows 2-7 once **more.**

Rows 56-62: Knit across.

Row 63 AND ALL WRONG SIDE ROWS THROUGH Row 117: K 13, purl across to next marker, (K7, purl across to next marker) twice, knit across.

Row 64: Knit across to second marker, K4, SSK, YO, K1, YO, K2 tog, (K3, SSK, YO, K1, YO, K2 tog) 4 times, knit across.

Row 66: Knit across to second marker, K5, YO, slip, slip, K1, P2SSO, YO, (K5, YO, slip, slip, K1, P2SSO, YO) 4 times, knit across.

Row 68: Repeat Row 64.

Row 70: Knit across to second marker, SSK, YO, K1, YO, K2 tog, (K3, SSK, YO, K1, YO, K2 tog) 5 times, knit across.

Row 72: Knit across to second marker, K1, YO, slip, slip, K1, P2SSO, YO, (K5, YO, slip, slip, K1, P2SSO, YO) 5 times, knit across.

Row 74: Repeat Row 70.

Rows 75-117: Repeat Rows 63-74, 3 times; then repeat Rows 63-69 once **more.**

Rows 118-124: Knit across.

Row 125: K 13, purl across to next marker, (K7, purl across to next marker) twice, knit across.

Rows 126-303: Repeat Rows 2-125 once, then repeat Rows 2-55 once **more**.

BORDER
Work in Garter Stitch for 2" (5 cm), ending by working a **wrong** side row.

Bind off all sts in knit.

Warm Bundle

■■□□ EASY

Design by Melissa Leapman

Finished Size: 35" x 46¹/₂" (89 cm x 118 cm)

MATERIALS

Medium Weight Yarn
  15¹/₂ ounces, 1,035 yards
    (440 grams, 946 meters)
  29" (73.5 cm) Circular knitting needles,
    sizes 9 (5.5 mm) **and** 10 (6 mm) **or**
    sizes needed for gauge
Yarn needle

GAUGE: With larger size needle,
      in pattern, 2 repeats (16 sts)
      and 20 rows = 4" (10 cm)

Techniques used:
• YO *(Figs. 4a & b, page 75)*
• K2 tog *(Fig. 8, page 76)*
• P2 tog *(Fig. 11, page 77)*
• P2 tog tbl *(Fig. 12, page 77)*
• SSK *(Figs. 10a-c, page 77)*
• M1 *(Figs. 6a & b, page 76)*
• M1P *(Figs. 7a & b, page 76)*

AFGHAN BODY

With larger size needle, cast on 129 sts.

Row 1: Purl across.

Row 2 (Right side)**:** Knit across.

Row 3: Purl across.

Row 4: K2, K2 tog, YO, K1, YO, SSK, (K3, K2 tog, YO, K1, YO, SSK) across to last 2 sts, K2.

Row 5: P1, (P2 tog tbl, YO, P3, YO, P2 tog, P1) across.

Row 6: Knit across.

Row 7: Purl across.

Repeat Rows 2-7 for pattern until Afghan Body measures approximately 43¹/₂" (110.5 cm) from cast on edge, ending by working Row 7.

Bind off all sts in knit.

MITERED EDGING

FIRST SIDE

With **right** side facing, using smaller size needle, and leaving a long end for sewing, pick up an odd number of stitches evenly spaced across bound off edge *(Fig. 21a, page 79)*.

Row 1 (Wrong side)**:** P2, K1, (P1, K1) across to last 2 sts, P2.

Row 2: K2, M1, P1, (K1, P1) across to last 2 sts, M1, K2.

Row 3: P3, K1, (P1, K1) across to last 3 sts, P3.

Row 4: K2, M1P, K1, (P1, K1) across to last 2 sts, M1P, K2.

Rows 5-9: Repeat Rows 1-4 once, then repeat Row 1 once **more**.

Bind off all sts in pattern.

SECOND SIDE

With **right** side facing, using smaller size needle, and leaving a long end for sewing, pick up an odd number of stitches evenly spaced across cast on edge.

Rows 1-9: Work same as First Side.

Bind off all sts in pattern.

THIRD AND FOURTH SIDES

With **right** side facing, using smaller size needle, and leaving a long end for sewing, pick up an odd number of stitches evenly spaced across long edge of Afghan Body *(Fig. 21b, page 79)*.

Rows 1-9: Work same as First Side.

Bind off all sts in pattern.

CORNER SEAMS

With **right** side facing, edges even, and using long end, sew through both sides once to secure the beginning of the seam. Inserting needle from **right** to **left**, catch one strand from each edge. Inserting needle from **left** to **right** on next row, catch one strand from each edge *(Fig. A)*. Continue in this manner to the end of the seam.

Fig. A

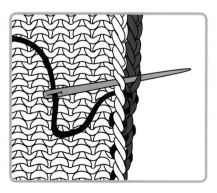

Sweet Hugs

■■□□ EASY

Design by Melissa Leapman

Finished Size: 37" x 47" (94 cm x 119.5 cm)

MATERIALS

Medium Weight Yarn
21 ounces, 1,400 yards
(600 grams, 1,280 meters)
29" (73.5 cm) Circular knitting needles,
sizes 9 (5.5 mm) **and** 10 (6 mm) **or**
sizes needed for gauge
Yarn needle

GAUGE: With larger size needle, in pattern,
2 repeats (12 sts) = 2$\frac{1}{2}$" (6.25 cm);
20 rows = 4" (10 cm)

Techniques used:
• YO *(Fig. 4a, page 75)*
• Slip, slip, K1, P2SSO *(Figs. 15a & b, page 78)*
• M1 *(Figs. 6a & b, page 76)*
• M1P *(Figs. 7a & b, page 76)*

AFGHAN BODY
With larger size needle, cast on 167 sts.

Row 1: Purl across.

Row 2 (Right side)**:** K1, P3, (K3, P3) across to last st, K1.

Row 3: P1, K3, (P3, K3) across to last st, P1.

Rows 4 and 5: Repeat Rows 2 and 3.

Row 6: K4, YO, slip, slip, K1, P2SSO, ★ YO, K3, YO, slip, slip, K1, P2SSO; repeat from ★ across to last 4 sts, YO, K4.

Row 7: P4, K3, (P3, K3) across to last 4 sts, P4.

Row 8: K4, P3, (K3, P3) across to last 4 sts, K4.

Rows 9-11: Repeat Rows 7 and 8 once, then repeat Row 7 once **more**.

Row 12: K1, YO, slip, slip, K1, P2SSO, ★ YO, K3, YO, slip, slip, K1, P2SSO; repeat from ★ across to last st, YO, K1.

Row 13: P1, K3, (P3, K3) across to last st, P1.

Row 14: K1, P3, (K3, P3) across to last st, K1.

Rows 15-17: Repeat Rows 13 and 14 once, then repeat Row 13 once **more**.

Repeat Rows 6-17 for pattern until Afghan Body measures approximately 44" (112 cm) from cast on edge, ending by working Row 11.

Bind off all sts in knit.

MITERED EDGING
Work same as Warm Bundle, page 50.

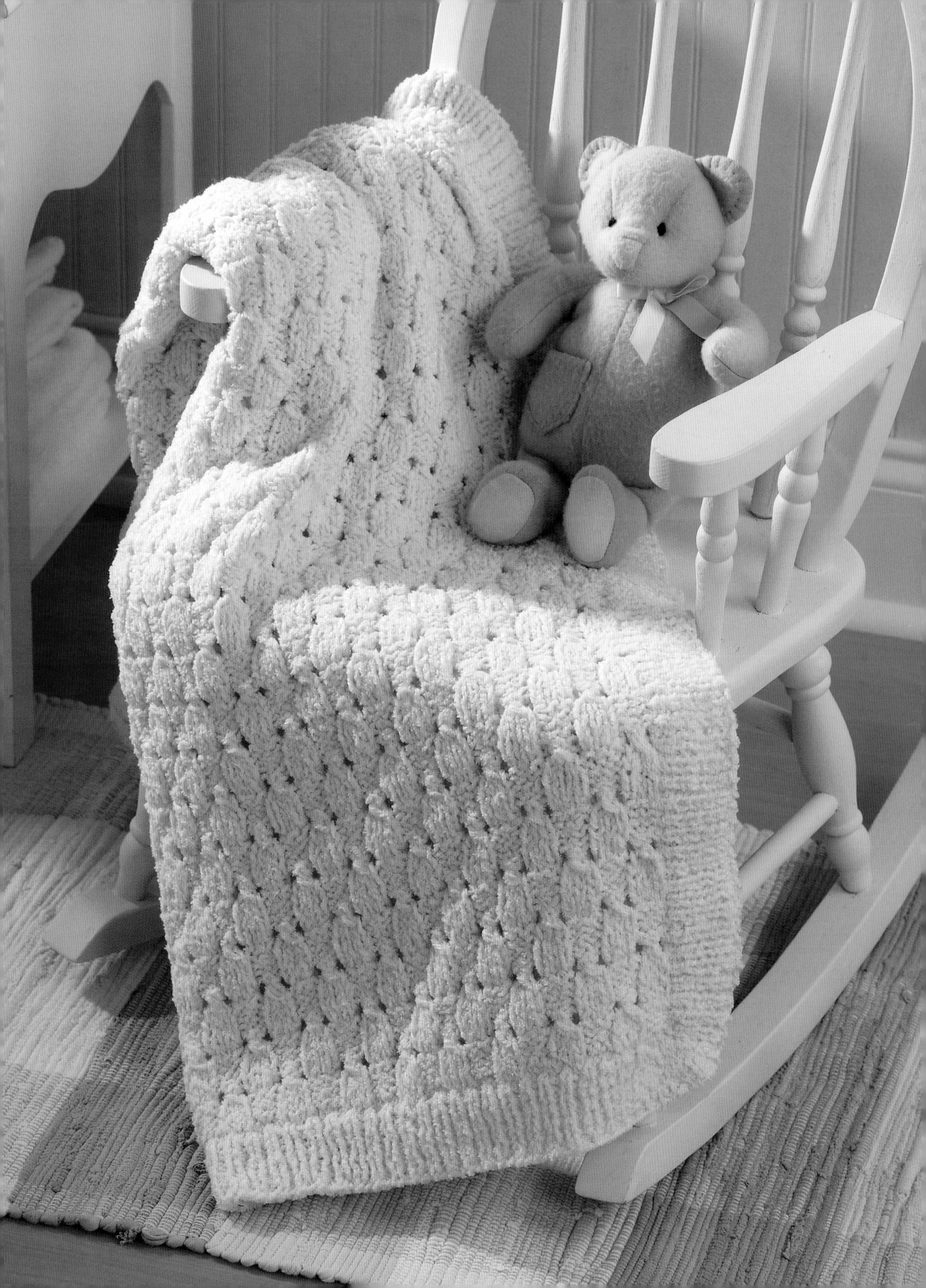

Tanya

■■■□ INTERMEDIATE

Design by Melissa Leapman

Finished Size: 35″ x 45″ (89 cm x 114.5 cm)

MATERIALS

Medium Weight Yarn

24¹/₂ ounces, 1,245 yards
 (700 grams, 1,138 meters)
29″ (73.5 cm) Circular knitting needle,
 size 9 (5.5 mm) **or** size needed for gauge

GAUGE: In Stockinette Stitch,
 17 sts and 22 rows = 4″ (10 cm)

Techniques used:
• YO *(Fig. 4a, page 75)*
• K2 tog *(Fig. 8, page 76)*
• SSK *(Figs. 10a-c, page 77)*

STITCH GUIDE

RIGHT TWIST

(abbreviated RT) (uses next 2 sts)
Knit second stitch on left needle *(Fig. A)* making sure **not** to drop off, then knit the first stitch *(Fig. B)* letting both sts drop off needle together.

Fig. A   Fig. B

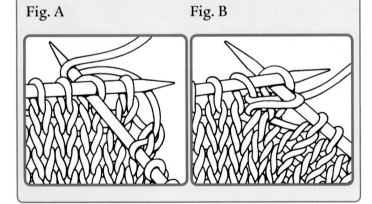

LEFT TWIST *(abbreviated LT)* (uses next 2 sts)
Working **behind** first st on left needle, knit into the back of second st *(Fig. C)* making sure **not** to drop off, then knit the first st *(Fig. D)* letting both sts drop off needle.

Fig. C   Fig. D

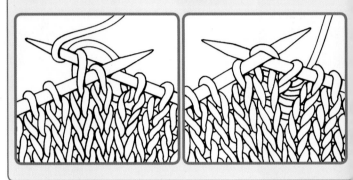

AFGHAN

Cast on 151 sts.

Rows 1-8: K1, (P1, K1) across.

Row 9 (Right side)**:** K1, (P1, K1) twice, P2, K3, K2 tog, YO, work LT, (K4, K2 tog, YO, work LT) across to last 9 sts, K2, P2, K1, (P1, K1) twice.

Row 10: K1, (P1, K1) 3 times, purl across to last 7 sts, K1, (P1, K1) 3 times.

Row 11: K1, (P1, K1) twice, P2, K2, work RT, YO, SSK (K4, work RT, YO, SSK) across to last 10 sts, K3, P2, K1, (P1, K1) twice.

Row 12: K1, (P1, K1) 3 times, purl across to last 7 sts, K1, (P1, K1) 3 times.

Repeat Rows 9-12 for pattern until Afghan measures approximately 43¹/₂″ (110.5 cm) from cast on edge, ending by working Row 12.

Last 8 Rows: K1, (P1, K1) across.

Bind off all sts in pattern.

◼◼◼◻ **INTERMEDIATE**   *Design by Melissa Leapman*

Finished Size: 35¹/₂" (90 cm) square

MATERIALS

Medium Weight Yarn
17¹/₂ ounces, 855 yards
(500 grams, 782 meters)
29" (73.5 cm) Circular knitting needle,
size 9 (5.5 mm) **or** size needed for gauge

GAUGE: In Stockinette Stitch,
17 sts and 22 rows = 4" (10 cm)

Techniques used:
• YO *(Fig. 4a, page 75)*
• K2 tog *(Fig. 8, page 76)*
• SSK *(Figs. 10a-c, page 77)*
• Slip 2 tog as if to **knit**, K1, P2SSO *(Figs. 16a & b, page 78)*

AFGHAN
Cast on 151 sts.

Rows 1-8: K1, (P1, K1) across.

Row 9 (Right side)**:** K1, (P1, K1) 3 times, (YO, SSK, K1, K2 tog, YO, K1) across to last 6 sts, (P1, K1) 3 times.

Row 10: K1, (P1, K1) twice, purl across to last 5 sts, K1, (P1, K1) twice.

Row 11: (K1, P1) 3 times, K2, YO, slip 2 tog, K1, P2SSO, (YO, K3, YO, slip 2 tog, K1, P2SSO) across to last 8 sts, YO, K2, (P1, K1) 3 times.

Row 12: K1, (P1, K1) twice, purl across to last 5 sts, K1, (P1, K1) twice.

Repeat Rows 9-12 for pattern until Afghan measures approximately 34" (86.5 cm) from cast on edge, ending by working Row 12.

Last 8 Rows: K1, (P1, K1) across.

Bind off all sts in pattern.

Three Color Chevron

◖■◻◻ **EASY**

Design by Donna Inman

Finished Size: 30″ x 40″ (76 cm x 101.5 cm)

MATERIALS

Medium Weight Yarn
  White - 6^1/$_2$ ounces, 425 yards
    (180 grams, 389 meters)
  Green and Yellow - 4^1/$_2$ ounces, 295 yards
    (130 grams, 270 meters) **each** color
  29″ (73.5 cm) Circular knitting needle,
    size 9 (5.5 mm) **or** size needed for gauge
  2 Stitch holders
  Yarn needle

GAUGE: In Garter Stitch, 16 sts = 4″ (10 cm)

Techniques used:
- YO *(Fig. 4a, page 75)*
- K2 tog *(Fig. 8, page 76)*

BOTTOM BORDER
With White, cast on 120 sts.

Rows 1-9: Knit across.

Row 10: K6, slip sts just worked onto st holder (Border), knit across to last 6 sts, slip last 6 sts onto second st holder (Border): 108 sts.

CENTER PANEL
Center Panel is worked in the following stripe sequence: 2 Rows White, ★ 4 rows **each** Green, Yellow, White; repeat from ★ for sequence.

Row 1 (Wrong side)**:** Purl across.

Row 2: ★ K2 tog twice, (YO, K1) 4 times, K2 tog twice; repeat from ★ across.

Rows 3 and 4: With next color, knit across.

Repeat Rows 1-4 for pattern until piece measures approximately 38^1/$_2$″ (98 cm) from cast on edge, ending by working Row 2 with White.

With yarn needle, thread a long length of yarn through remaining sts; tie ends together.

SIDE BORDER
With **wrong** side facing, slip sts from left side st holder onto needle. With White, knit every row until Border measures same as Center Panel, ending by working a **right** side row; slip sts onto st holder.

Sew Border to Center Panel.

With **right** side facing, work second Side Border same as first side.

TOP BORDER
With **wrong** side facing, slip all sts onto needle.

Rows 1-9: With White, knit across.

Bind off all sts in knit.

Square Rainbow

Design by Marion Graham

Finished Size: 33" (84 cm) square

MATERIALS
Medium Weight Yarn
  White - 11^1/$_2$ ounces, 590 yards
    (330 grams, 539 meters)
  Purple - 3 ounces, 155 yards
    (100 grams, 142 meters)
  Blue - 2^1/$_2$ ounces, 130 yards
    (70 grams, 119 meters)
  Green - 2 ounces, 100 yards
    (60 grams, 91 meters)
  Yellow - 1^1/$_2$ ounces, 75 yards
    (40 grams, 69 meters)
  Pink - 1 ounce, 50 yards
    (30 grams, 46 meters)
Straight knitting needles, size 9 (5.5 mm) **or** size
  needed for gauge
Yarn needle

GAUGE: In Garter Stitch,
    16 sts and 32 rows = 4" (10 cm)

Technique used:
• Knit increase *(Figs. 5a & b, page 76)*

STRIPE SEQUENCE
Alternate 12 rows of White with 12 rows **each** of Pink,
Yellow, Green, Blue, and Purple, ending by working
12 rows of White.

PANEL (Make 4)
With White, cast on 3 sts.

Row 1 (Right side)**:** Work knit increase twice,
K1: 5 sts.

Row 2: Knit across.

Row 3 (Increase row)**:** Work knit increase, knit across
to last 2 sts, work knit increase, K1: 7 sts.

Row 4: Knit across.

Rows 5-12: Repeat Rows 3 and 4, 4 times: 15 sts.

When changing colors, always leave a 10" (25.5 cm)
strand of yarn for weaving the seam.

Rows 13-132: Working in Stripe Sequence, repeat
Rows 3 and 4 for pattern: 135 sts.

Bind off all sts **very loosely.**

FINISHING
Afghan is assembled by weaving the 4 Panels together
as follows:
Hold edges together with **right** sides facing you.
Weave seam catching one stitch from each edge
(Fig. A) and being careful to match rows.

Fig. A

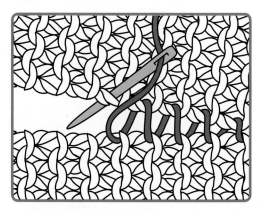

Webbed

Design by Jeannine LaRoche

Finished Size: 35″ x 36″ (89 cm x 91.5 cm)

MATERIALS

Light Weight Yarn

White - 6¹/₂ ounces, 595 yards
   (180 grams, 544 meters)
Green - 4¹/₂ ounces, 410 yards
   (130 grams, 375 meters)
29″ (73.5 cm) Circular knitting needle, size 7
   (4.5 mm) **or** size needed for gauge

GAUGE: In pattern, 20 sts and 28 rows = 4″ (10 cm)

Techniques used:
- Knit increase *(Figs. 5a & b, page 76)*
- YO *(Fig. 4a, page 75)*
- K2 tog *(Fig. 8, page 76)*

AFGHAN
With Green, cast on 150 sts.

Rows 1-5: Knit across.

Row 6: K9, work knit increase, (K5, work knit increase) across to last 8 sts, K8: 173 sts.

When instructed to slip a stitch, always slip as if to purl.

To avoid cutting yarn, carry yarn not being used loosely along edge, twisting every other row on wrong side, one stitch in.

Row 7 (Right side): With White K5, (slip 1, K5) across.

Row 8: K5, WYF slip 1, (P5, slip 1) across to last 5 sts, K5.

Rows 9 and 10: Repeat Rows 7 and 8.

Rows 11 and 12: With Green, knit across.

Repeat Rows 7-12 for pattern until Afghan measures approximately 35″ (89 cm) from cast on edge, ending by working Row 10.

Decrease Row: With Green K9, K2 tog, (K5, K2 tog) across to last 8 sts, K8: 150 sts.

Next 5 Rows: Knit across.

Bind off all sts in knit.

Winsome White

Design by Carole Prior

Finished Size: 34″ x 45″ (86.5 cm x 114.5 cm)

MATERIALS

Medium Weight Yarn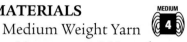

32 ounces, 1,865 yards
  (910 grams, 1,705 meters)
29″ (73.5 cm) Circular knitting needle,
  size 10¹/₂ (6.5 mm) **or** size needed for gauge

Afghan is worked holding two strands of yarn together.

GAUGE: In pattern,
  11 sts and 15 rows = 3¹/₂″ (9 cm)

Techniques used:

- YO (*Fig. 4a, page 75*)
- K2 tog (*Fig. 8, page 76*)

AFGHAN

Cast on 107 sts.

Rows 1-6: Knit across.

Row 7: K4, purl across to last 4 sts, K4.

Row 8 (Right side)**:** K6, K2 tog, (YO, K2, K2 tog) across to last 7 sts, YO, K7.

Row 9: K4, purl across to last 4 sts, K4.

Row 10: Knit across.

Row 11: K4, purl across to last 4 sts, K4.

Row 12: K4, K2 tog, (YO, K2, K2 tog) across to last 5 sts, YO, K5.

Row 13: K4, purl across to last 4 sts, K4.

Row 14: Knit across.

Row 15: K4, purl across to last 4 sts, K4.

Repeat Rows 8-15 for pattern until Afghan measures approximately 44″ (112 cm) from cast on edge, ending by working Row 9 or Row 13.

Last 6 Rows: Knit across.

Bind off all sts in knit.

Wonderfully White

EASY +

Design by Carole Prior

Finished Size: 39″ x 45″ (99 cm x 114.5 cm)

MATERIALS

Medium Weight Yarn
   32 ounces, 1,865 yards
      (910 grams, 1,705 meters)
   29″ (73.5 cm) Circular knitting needles,
      sizes 10½ (6.5 mm) **and** 11 (8 mm) **or** sizes
      needed for gauge

Afghan is worked holding two strands of yarn together.

GAUGE: In pattern,
      11 sts and 15 rows = 3½″ (9 cm)

Techniques used:
- YO *(Figs. 4c & d, page 75)*
- K2 tog *(Fig. 8, page 76)*
- Slip 1 as if to **knit**, K2 tog, PSSO *(Figs. 14a & b, page 78)*

AFGHAN
With smaller size needle, cast on 125 sts.

Rows 1-5: Knit across.

Change to larger size needle.

Row 6 (Right side)**:** K4, P1, (K3, P1) across to last 4 sts, K4.

Row 7: K5, P3, (K1, P3) across to last 5 sts, K5.

Row 8: K4, P1, (YO, slip 1, K2 tog, PSSO, YO, P1) across to last 4 sts, K4.

Row 9: K5, P3, (K1, P3) across to last 5 sts, K5.

Repeat Rows 6-9 for pattern until Afghan measures approximately 44″ (112 cm) from cast on edge, ending by working Row 9.

Change to smaller size needle.

Last 6 Rows: Knit across.

Bind off all sts in knit.

Baby Dots

EASY

Design by Kay Meadors

Finished Size: 36″ x 41″ (91.5 cm x 104 cm)

MATERIALS

Light Weight Yarn

White - 21¹/₂ ounces, 1,980 yards
(610 grams, 1,811 meters)
Pink - 1¹/₂ ounces, 140 yards
(40 grams, 128 meters)
Blue - 1¹/₂ ounces, 140 yards
(40 grams, 128 meters)
Yellow - 1¹/₂ ounces, 140 yards
(40 grams, 128 meters)
Green - 1¹/₂ ounces, 140 yards
(40 grams, 128 meters)
29″ (73.5 cm) Circular knitting needles,
sizes 10 (6 mm) **and** 10¹/₂ (6.5 mm) **or**
size needed for gauge

Entire Afghan is worked holding two strands of yarn
together.

GAUGE: With larger size needle,
in pattern, 11 sts = 3″ (7.5 cm)
and 26 rows = 4″ (10 cm)

AFGHAN

With smaller size needle and White, cast on 133 sts.

Rows 1-7: Knit across.

Change to larger size needle.

Row 8 (Right side)**:** Knit across.

Row 9: K4, purl across to last 4 sts, K4.

Rows 10 and 11: Repeat Rows 8 and 9.

Both side borders of Afghan are worked at the
same time, using separate yarn for **each** side. When
instructed to slip a stitch, always slip as if to **purl.**

Row 12: K4 (side border), drop White *(Fig. 20,
page 79)*; with Pink K1, (slip 1, K1) across to last 4 sts,
drop Pink; with next White K4 (side border).

Row 13: K4, WYF drop White; with Pink K1,
(WYF slip 1, WYB K1) across to last 4 sts, WYF cut
Pink; with next White K4.

Row 14: Knit across to last 4 sts, drop White; with
next White K4.

Row 15: K4, WYF drop White; with next White purl
across to last 4 sts, K4.

Rows 16 and 17: Repeat Rows 14 and 15.

Row 18: K4, drop White; with Blue K2, slip 1, (K1,
slip 1) across to last 6 sts, K2, drop Blue; with next
White K4.

Row 19: K4, WYF drop White; with Blue K2,
WYF slip 1, (WYB K1, WYF slip 1) across to last 6 sts,
WYB K2, WYF cut Blue; with next White K4.

Row 20: Knit across to last 4 sts, drop White; with
next White K4.

Row 21: K4, WYF drop White; with next White purl
across to last 4 sts, K4.

Rows 22 and 23: Repeat Rows 20 and 21.

Row 24: K4, drop White; with Yellow K1, (slip 1, K1)
across to last 4 sts, drop Yellow; with next White K4.

Row 25: K4, WYF drop White; with Yellow K1,
(WYF slip 1, WYB K1) across to last 4 sts, WYF cut
Yellow; with next White K4.

Instructions continued on page 7.

Garland

INTERMEDIATE

Design by Cynthia Guggemos

Finished Size: 35″ (89 cm) square

MATERIALS

Light Weight Yarn
  14 ounces, 1,150 yards
    (400 grams, 1,052 meters)
  29″ (73.5 cm) Circular knitting needle,
    size 6 (4 mm) **or** size needed for gauge
  Markers

GAUGE: In Stockinette Stitch,
        22 sts and 30 rows = 4″ (10 cm)

Techniques used:
- YO *(Fig. 4a, page 75)*
- K2 tog *(Fig. 8, page 76)*
- SSK *(Figs. 10a-c, page 77)*
- M1 *(Figs. 6a & b, page 76)*
- Slip 1 as if to **knit**, K2 tog, PSSO *(Figs. 14a & b, page 78)*

BOTTOM EDGING

Cast on 169 sts.

Rows 1-19: Knit across.

Row 20 (Right side)**:** K 12, place marker *(see Markers, page 74)*, knit across to last 12 sts, place marker, knit across.

Row 21: Knit across to next marker, purl across to next marker, knit across.

Row 22: Knit across to next marker, K1, (YO, K2 tog) across to next marker, knit across.

Row 23: Knit across to next marker, purl across to next marker, knit across.

Rows 24-26: Knit across.

BOTTOM BAND

Row 1: Knit across to next marker, purl across to next marker, knit across.

Row 2: Knit across to next marker, K3, YO, slip 1, K2 tog, PSSO, (YO, K5, YO, slip 1, K2 tog, PSSO) across to within 3 sts of next marker, YO, knit across.

Row 3: Knit across to next marker, purl across to next marker, knit across.

Row 4: Knit across to next marker, K1, (K2 tog, YO, K3, YO, SSK, K1) across to next marker, knit across.

Repeat Rows 1-4 for pattern until Afghan measures approximately 9¼″ (23.5 cm) from cast on edge, ending by working Row 3.

CENTER

Row 1: Knit across to next marker, K1, (K2 tog, YO, K3, YO, SSK, K1) 4 times, place marker, K7, (M1, K8) 9 times, place marker, (K1, K2 tog, YO, K3, YO, SSK) 4 times, knit across: 178 sts.

Row 2: Knit across to next marker, purl across to last marker, knit across.

Row 3: ★ Knit across to next marker, K3, YO, slip 1, K2 tog, PSSO, YO, (K5, YO, slip 1, K2 tog, PSSO, YO) 3 times, K3; repeat from ★ once **more**, knit across.

Row 4: Knit across to next marker, purl across to last marker, knit across.

Row 5: ★ Knit across to next marker, K1, (K2 tog, YO, K3, YO, SSK, K1) 4 times; repeat from ★ once **more**, knit across.

Repeat Rows 2-5 for pattern until Afghan measures approximately 25¾″ (65.5 cm) from cast on edge, ending by working Row 4.

Instructions continued on page 72

Garland

Continued from page 70.

TOP BAND

Row 1: Knit across to next marker, K1, (K2 tog, YO, K3, YO, SSK, K1) 4 times, remove marker, K7, (K2 tog, K7) 9 times, remove marker, (K1, K2 tog, YO, K3, YO, SSK) 4 times, knit across: 169 sts.

Row 2: Knit across to next marker, purl across to next marker, knit across.

Row 3: Knit across to next marker, K3, YO, slip 1, K2 tog, PSSO, (YO, K5, YO, slip 1, K2 tog, PSSO) across to within 3 sts of next marker, YO, knit across.

Row 4: Knit across to next marker, purl across to next marker, knit across.

Row 5: Knit across to next marker, K1, (K2 tog, YO, K3, YO, SSK, K1) across to next marker, knit across.

Repeat Rows 2-5 for pattern until Afghan measures approximately 32^1/$_2$" (82.5 cm) from cast on edge, ending by working a **wrong** side row.

TOP EDGING

Rows 1-3: Knit across.

Row 4: Knit across to next marker, purl across to next marker, knit across.

Row 5: Knit across to next marker, K1, (YO, K2 tog) across to next marker, knit across.

Row 6: Knit across to next marker, purl across to next marker, knit across.

Rows 7-24: Knit across.

Bind off all sts in knit.

Baby Dots

Continued from page 68.

Rows 26-29: Repeat Rows 20-23.

Row 30: K4, drop White; with Green K2, slip 1, (K1, slip 1) across to last 6 sts, K2, drop Green; with next White K4.

Row 31: K4, WYF drop White; with Green K2, WYF slip 1, (WYB K1, WYF slip 1) across to last 6 sts, WYB K2, WYF cut Green; with next White K4.

Rows 32-35: Repeat Rows 20-23.

Row 36: K4, drop White; with Pink K1, (slip 1, K1) across to last 4 sts, drop Pink; with next White K4.

Row 37: K4, WYF drop White; with Pink K1, (WYF slip 1, WYB K1) across to last 4 sts, WYF cut Pink; with next White K4.

Rows 38-253: Repeat Rows 14-37, 9 times.

Row 254: Knit across to last 4 sts, cut White; with next White K4.

Row 255: K4, purl across to last 4 sts, K4.

Row 256: Knit across.

Change to smaller size needle.

Rows 257-263: Knit across.

Bind off all sts in knit.

ABBREVIATIONS

ch(s)	chain(s)
cm	centimeters
dc	double crochet(s)
K	knit
LT	Left Twist
M1	Make One
M1P	Make One Purl
mm	millimeters
P	purl
PSSO	pass slipped stitch over
P2SSO	pass 2 slipped stitches over
Rnd(s)	Round(s)
RT	Right Twist
RT2	Right Twist 2
sc	single crochet(s)
SSK	slip, slip, knit
st(s)	stitch(es)
tbl	through back loop
tog	together
WYB	with yarn back
WYF	with yarn forward
YO	yarn over

★ — work instructions following ★ as many **more** times as indicated in addition to the first time.

† to † — work all instructions from first † to second † **as many** times as specified.

( ) or [ ] — work enclosed instructions **as many** times as specified by the number immediately following **or** work all enclosed instructions in the stitch indicated **or** contains explanatory remarks.

colon (:) — the number given after a colon at the end of a row or round denotes the number of stitches you should have on that row or round.

KNIT TERMINOLOGY	
UNITED STATES	**INTERNATIONAL**
gauge =	tension
bind off =	cast off
yarn over (YO) =	yarn forward (yfwd) **or** yarn around needle (yrn)

Yarn Weight Symbol & Names	LACE 0	SUPER FINE 1	FINE 2	LIGHT 3	MEDIUM 4	BULKY 5	SUPER BULKY 6
Type of Yarns in Category	Fingering, size 10 crochet thread	Sock, Fingering, Baby	Sport, Baby	DK, Light Worsted	Worsted, Afghan, Aran	Chunky, Craft, Rug	Bulky, Roving
Knit Gauge Range* in Stockinette St to 4" (10 cm)	33-40** sts	27-32 sts	23-26 sts	21-24 sts	16-20 sts	12-15 sts	6-11 sts
Advised Needle Size Range	000-1	1 to 3	3 to 5	5 to 7	7 to 9	9 to 11	11 and larger

*GUIDELINES ONLY: The chart above reflects the most commonly used gauges and needle sizes for specific yarn categories.

** Lace weight yarns are usually knitted on larger needles to create lacy openwork patterns. Accordingly, a gauge range is difficult to determine. Always follow the gauge stated in your pattern.

KNITTING NEEDLES																
U.S.	0	1	2	3	4	5	6	7	8	9	10	10½	11	13	15	17
U.K.	13	12	11	10	9	8	7	6	5	4	3	2	1	00	000	---
Metric - mm	2	2.25	2.75	3.25	3.5	3.75	4	4.5	5	5.5	6	6.5	8	9	10	12.75

◖◻◻◻ **BEGINNER**	Projects for first-time knitters using basic knit and purl stitches. Minimal shaping.	
◖■◻◻ **EASY**	Projects using basic stitches, repetitive stitch patterns, simple color changes, and simple shaping and finishing.	
◖■■◻ **INTERMEDIATE**	Projects with a variety of stitches, such as basic cables and lace, simple intarsia, double-pointed needles and knitting in the round needle techniques, mid-level shaping and finishing.	
◖■■■ **EXPERIENCED**	Projects using advanced techniques and stitches, such as short rows, fair isle, more intricate intarsia, cables, lace patterns, and numerous color changes.	

GAUGE

Exact gauge is **essential** for proper size. Before beginning your Afghan, make a sample swatch in the yarn and needle specified. After completing the swatch, measure it, counting your stitches and rows carefully. If your swatch is larger or smaller than specified, **make another, changing needle size to get the correct gauge**. Keep trying until you find the size needles that will give you the specified gauge. Once proper gauge is obtained, measure width of Afghan approximately every 3″ (7.5 cm) to be sure gauge remains consistent.

YARN

The Afghans in this leaflet were made using a variety of yarns. Any brand of the specified weight of yarn may be used. It is best to refer to the yardage/meters to determine how many balls, skeins, or hanks to purchase. Remember, in order for your Afghan to be the correct size, it is not the brand of yarn that matters, but the GAUGE/TENSION that is important.

MARKERS

As a convenience to you, we have used markers to help distinguish the beginning of a pattern. Place markers as instructed. You may use purchased markers or tie a length of contrasting color yarn around the needle. When you reach a marker on each row, slip it from the left needle to the right needle; remove it when no longer needed.

BASIC PATTERN STITCHES
STOCKINETTE STITCH

Knit one row or number of stitches indicated (right side), purl one row or number of stitches indicated. The knit side is smooth and flat *(Fig. 1a)*, and the purl side is bumpy *(Fig. 1b)*.

Fig. 1a   Fig. 1b

GARTER STITCH

Knit every row. Two rows of knitting make one horizontal ridge in your fabric (*Fig. 2*).

Fig. 2

SEED STITCH

Knit the purl stitches and purl the knit stitches as they face you (*Fig. 3*).

Fig. 3

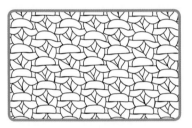

YARN OVERS

After a knit stitch, before a knit stitch

Bring the yarn forward **between** the needles, then back **over** the top of the right hand needle, so that it is now in position to knit the next stitch (*Fig. 3a*).

Fig. 4a

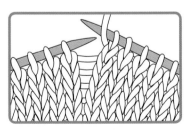

After a purl stitch, before a purl stitch

Take the yarn **over** the right hand needle to the back, then forward **under** it, so that it is now in position to purl the next stitch (*Fig. 4b*).

Fig. 4b

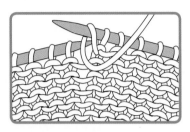

After a knit stitch, before a purl stitch

Bring the yarn forward **between** the needles, then back **over** the top of the right hand needle and forward **between** the needles again, so that it is now in position to purl the next stitch (*Fig. 4c*).

Fig. 4c

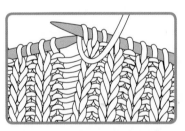

After a purl stitch, before a knit stitch

Take the yarn **over** the right hand needle to the back, so that it is now in position to knit the next stitch (*Fig. 4d*).

Fig. 4d

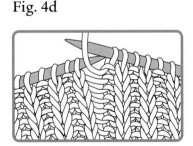

INCREASES

KNIT INCREASE (uses one st)

Knit the next stitch but do **not** slip the old stitch off the left needle *(Fig. 5a)*. Insert the right needle into the **back** loop of the **same** stitch and knit it *(Fig. 5b)*, then slip the old stitch off the left needle.

Fig. 5a   Fig. 5b

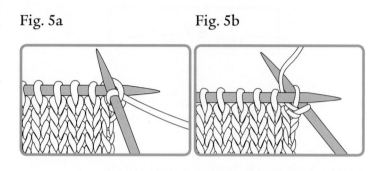

MAKE ONE (abbreviated M1)

Insert the **left** needle under the horizontal strand between the stitches from the **front** *(Fig. 6a)*. Then knit into the **back** of the strand *(Fig. 6b)*.

Fig. 6a   Fig. 6b

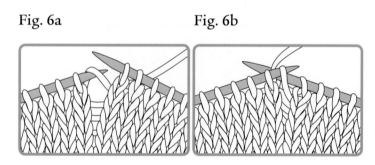

MAKE ONE PURL (abbreviated M1P)

Insert the **left** needle under the horizontal strand between the stitches from the **back** *(Fig. 7a)*. Then purl the strand *(Fig. 7b)*.

Fig. 7a   Fig. 7b

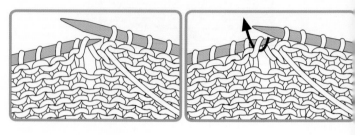

DECREASES

KNIT 2 TOGETHER (abbreviated K2 tog)

Insert the right needle into the **front** of the first two stitches on the left needle as if to **knit** *(Fig. 8)*, then knit them together as if they were one stitch.

Fig. 8

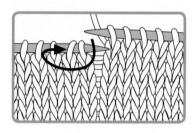

SLIP 1, KNIT 1, PASS SLIPPED STITCH OVER *(abbreviated slip 1, K1, PSSO)*

Slip one stitch as if to **knit**. Knit the next stitch. With the left needle, bring the slipped stitch over the knit stitch *(Fig. 9)* and off the needle.

Fig. 9

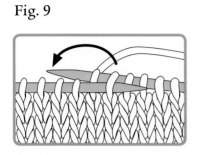

SLIP, SLIP, KNIT *(abbreviated SSK)*

With yarn in back of work, separately slip two stitches as if to **knit** *(Fig. 10a)*. Insert the **left** needle into the **front** of both slipped stitches *(Fig. 10b)* and knit them together *(Fig. 10c)*.

Fig. 10a   Fig. 10b

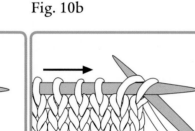

Fig. 10c

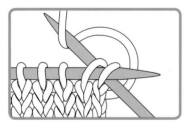

PURL 2 TOGETHER *(abbreviated P2 tog)*

Insert the right needle into the **front** of the first two stitches on the left needle as if to **purl** *(Fig. 11)*, then purl them together as if they were one stitch.

Fig. 11

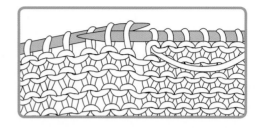

PURL 2 TOGETHER THROUGH THE BACK LOOP *(abbreviated P2 tog tbl)*

Insert the right needle into the **back** of both stitches from **back** to **front** *(Fig. 12)*, then purl them together as if they were one stitch.

Fig. 12

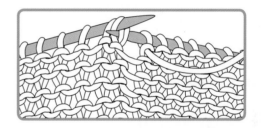

SLIP 1, KNIT 2, PASS SLIPPED STITCH OVER *(abbreviated slip 1, K2, PSSO)*

Slip one stitch as if to **knit** *(Fig. 13a)*, then knit the next two stitches. With the left needle, bring the slipped stitch over the two stitches just worked *(Fig. 13b)* and off the needle.

Fig. 13a   Fig. 13b

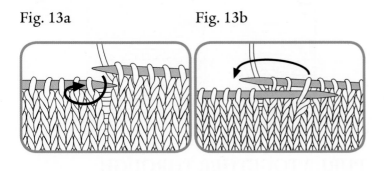

SLIP 1, KNIT 2 TOGETHER, PASS SLIPPED STITCH OVER *(abbreviated slip 1, K2 tog, PSSO)*

Slip one stitch as if to **knit** *(Fig. 14a)*, then knit the next two stitches together *(Fig. 8, page 76)*. With the left needle, bring the slipped stitch over the stitch just made *(Fig. 14b)* and off the needle.

Fig. 14a   Fig. 14b

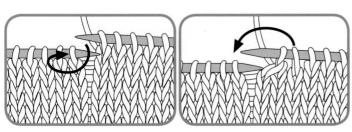

SLIP, SLIP, K1, PASS 2 SLIPPED STITCHES OVER *(abbreviated slip, slip, K1, P2SSO)*

With yarn in back, separately slip two stitches as if to **knit** *(Fig. 15a)*, then knit the next stitch. With the left needle, bring both slipped stitches over the knit stitch *(Fig. 15b)* and off the needle.

Fig. 15a   Fig. 15b

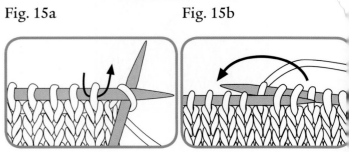

SLIP 2 TOGETHER, KNIT 1, PASS 2 SLIPPED STITCHES OVER *(abbreviated slip 2 tog, K1, P2SSO)*

Slip two stitches together as if to **knit** *(Fig. 16a)*, then knit the next stitch. With the left needle, bring the two slipped stitches over the stitch just made *(Fig. 16b)* and off the needle.

Fig. 16a   Fig. 16b

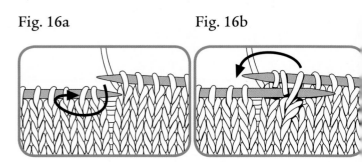

KNIT 3 TOGETHER *(abbreviated K3 tog)*

Insert the right needle into the **front** of the first three stitches on the left needle as if to **knit** *(Fig. 17)*, then knit them together as if they were one stitch.

Fig. 17

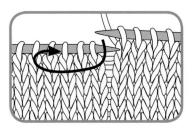

PURL 3 TOGETHER *(abbreviated P3 tog)*

Insert the right needle into the **front** of the first three stitches on the left needle as if to **purl** *(Fig. 18)*, then purl them together as if they were one stitch.

Fig. 18

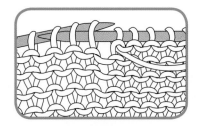

SLIP 2 TOGETHER, KNIT 3 TOGETHER, PASS 2 SLIPPED STITCHES OVER

(abbreviated slip 2, K3 tog, P2SSO)

Slip two stitches together as if to **knit** *(Fig. 19a)*, then knit the next three stitches together *(Fig. 17)*. With the left needle, bring the two slipped stitches over the stitch just made *(Fig. 19b)* and off the needle.

Fig. 19a   Fig. 19b

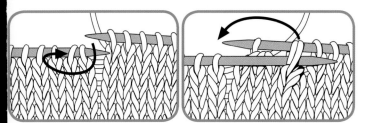

CHANGING COLORS

When changing colors, always pick up the new color yarn from **beneath** the dropped yarn and keep the color that has just been worked to the left of the new yarn *(Fig. 20)*. This will prevent holes in the finished afghan. Take extra care to keep your tension even. Cut yarn when no longer needed.

Fig. 20

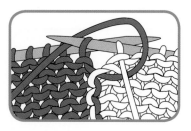

PICKING UP STITCHES

When instructed to pick up stitches, insert the needle from the **front** to the **back** under two strands at the edge of the worked piece *(Figs. 21a & b)*. Put the yarn around the needle as if to **knit**, then bring the needle with the yarn back through the stitch to the right side, resulting in a stitch on the needle.

Repeat this along the edge, picking up the required number of stitches.

A crochet hook may be helpful to pull yarn through.

Fig. 21a   Fig. 21b

BASIC CROCHET STITCHES

CHAIN *(abbreviated ch)*

To work a chain stitch, begin with a slip knot on the hook. Bring the yarn **over** the hook from back to front, catching the yarn with the hook and turning the hook slightly toward you to keep the yarn from slipping off. Draw the yarn through the slip knot *(Fig. 22)* (first chain st made).

Fig. 22

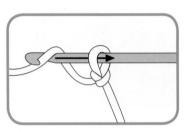

SLIP STITCH *(abbreviated slip st)*

To work a slip stitch, insert the hook in stitch indicated, YO and draw through st and through loop on hook *(Fig. 23)* (slip st made).

Fig. 23

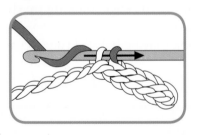

SINGLE CROCHET *(abbreviated sc)*

Insert the hook in stitch indicated, YO and pull up a loop, YO and draw through both loops on hook *(Fig. 24)* (single crochet made).

Fig. 24

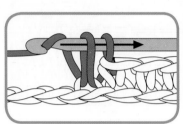

DOUBLE CROCHET *(abbreviated dc)*

YO, insert the hook in stitch indicated, YO and pull up a loop (3 loops on hook), YO and draw through 2 loops on hook *(Fig. 25a)*, YO and draw through remaining 2 loops on hook *(Fig. 25b)* (**double crochet made**).

Fig. 25a   Fig. 25b

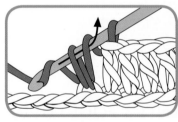